The Untold History of Canada

# OUR FORGOTTEN STRUGGLE FOR PROGRESS

## 1945-1972

Matthew J.L. Ehret

*With a special contribution by Richard Saunders*

Matthew J.L. Ehret
Visit my website at www.canadianpatriot.org

Printed in Canada

First Printing: December 2018
Canadian Patriot Press

ISBN 9781097746569

The cover features an image of Daniel Johnson Sr., and Charles de Gaulle during the latter's 1967 tour of Quebec. Also featured is a close-up of Canada's Prime Minister John Diefenbaker (1957-2963) and the Manicouagan 5 dam (Aka: The Daniel Johnson Dam) which largely represents Quebec's leap from a feudal society to an advanced engineering culture.

## *Dedication*

To all those whom I love and who share my hope in a beautiful future for mankind.

# CONTENTS

# PREFACE

The following chapters were written as a follow up to a series of studies on Canadian history focusing on the period of 1774-1789 written by Pierre Beaudry and published in the 2013 manuscript *"Canada: Republic or Colony"* [1]. These works were re-published as the first volume of the Untold History of Canada series in 2018. *Professor* Beaudry's studies begin with the posing of a singular question: Why did Canada fail to become the 14th colony of the Americas to rebel against the British Empire in 1776 in spite of the intensive organizing by Benjamin Franklin among others?

The work which has resulted from these studies and featured in the Untold History of Canada series are nothing less than a total reconstruction of Canadian history from 1774 to the present. Other discoveries in the field of Universal History which made this project possible include Graham Lowry's How the Nation Was Won (1988) [2], Anton Chaitkin's Treason in America: From Aaron Burr to Averill Harimann (1985) [3], Robert Ingraham's Manhattan's Struggle for Freedom Against the Slave Power of Virginia (2014) [4], Gerald Therrien's Unveiling of Canadian History (2015-2018) [5], Allen Salisbury's Civil War and the American System (1978) [6], and Lyndon LaRouche's Economics as History (2009) [7].

In this third volume of the series, we introduce the story of several leading nation builders of the 20th century whose lives and struggle have been obscured by establishment historians. We document for the first time in one location the interconnected networks of B.C.'s Premier W.A.C. Bennett, Canada's "Minister of Everything" C.D. Howe, Prime Minister John Diefenbaker, and Quebec's Premiers Maurice Duplessis, Paul Sauve and Daniel Johnson who were all aided by republican leaders of America and France during the post WWII period. These figures conducted a battle with the Rhodes Scholar-infested networks which have come to be known as the Deep State in our modern era, and in spite of their limitations, these figures all distinguished themselves by their genuine patriotism and love of scientific and technological progress.

Providing an additional dimension to this story of Canada's untold history, researcher Richard Saunders has contributed a chapter entitled "The Ugly Truth of General Andrew Macnaughton". This important research ties into the Canadian aspect of the assassination of John F. Kennedy and sabotaging of the great North American Water and Power Alliance in a surprising manner as the myth of the heroic Macnaughton is put to rest.

## Notes to Preface

[1] Pierre Beaudry's referenced work can be found in Canada: Republic or Colony: Canadian Patriot Special Report 2012 and in volume one of the Untold History of Canada (*The Tragic Consequences of the Quebec Act of 1774*), Canadian Patriot Press, 2018

[2] Graham Lowry, *How the Nation Was Won: America's Untold Story 1630-1754*, 1988

[3] Anton Chaitkin, *Treason in America: From Aaron Burr to Averill Harimann*, 1985

[4] Bob Ingraham, *Manhattan's Struggle for Human Freedom Against the Slave Power of Virginia*, EIR May 8, 2015

[5] Gerald Therrien, *The Unveiling of Canadian History*, published on the Canadian Patriot Review, 2015-2018

[6] Allen Salisbury, *The Civil War and the American System: America's Battle with Britain 1860-1876*, 1st printing. 1978

[7] Lyndon LaRouche, *Economics as History: The Science of Physical* Economy, Executive Intelligence Review, September 18, 2009

# A NEW METHOD FOR STUDYING UNIVERSAL HISTORY

*"The state itself is never the purpose, it is important only as the condition under which the purpose of mankind may be fulfilled, and this purpose of mankind is none other than the development of all the powers of people, i.e., progress. If the constitution of a state hinders the progress of the mind, it is contemptible and harmful, however well thought-out it may otherwise be... In general, we can establish a rule for judging political institutions, that they are only good and laudable, to the extent that they bring all forces inherent in persons to flourish, to the extent that they promote the progress of culture, or at least not hinder it. This rule applies to religious laws as well as to political ones: both are contemptible if they constrain a power of the human mind, if they impose upon the mind any sort of stagnation."*

*-Frederick Schiller, poet, dramatist and founder of the Science of Universal History, excerpted from his lecture on the Constitutions of Lycurgus' Sparta and Solon's Athens*

# INTRODUCTION

I can only imagine that as you pick up this book which is part of the "Untold History of Canada" series you may be asking yourself, *"well this author seems to be saying that they know something which they profess to be true and new about Canada... but how could anything new be said of a subject which has been dissected and chronicled by hundreds of thousands of authors for over 150 years? How is it possible that historical truths can even be known when history books are invariably written by the winners? What makes this version of Canada's history so different from everything that came before?"*

In answering these questions, I say that if we only had history books to work with, then the answer to the first question would be a definitive "No. Truth could never thus be known in history". However, if we recognize that history is not a mere collection of facts in books, but is rather a *process* shaped by individual personalities motivated by IDEAS of humanity and nature which are either right or wrong, and if these individuals played driving roles in the unfolding of history, then certainly we have much more than text books to work with.

In the course of human history, certain singular periods jump out from the monotonous flow of day to day events. At times of crisis, patterns of behaviour, norms and customs no longer work, systems break down and the civilization in question either transforms to something new and better, or collapses into what some have called dark ages.

Should a transformation to something better occur, then we will often discover that such a society was fortunate enough that a prophet had appeared among them. Such a prophet, though often hated and misunderstood in his own lifetime, will often provide the creative energy, leadership and cognitive dissonance necessary to break that society out of its complacency and free from the doomed pattern of behaviour which only served to perpetuate the social structures of an encrusted elite on the one hand while rendering the lives of the masses useless on the other.

Examples of such prophets and poets shine as beacons of light in a dark abyss, whose lives we can say in hindsight were completely necessary for the continuity of society's collective evolution. From Socrates and his student Plato who founded an academy dedicated to the perfectibility of mankind in Ancient Athens, to Confucius and his student Mencius who did the same in China, it matters not from what particular civilization these individuals arise, the cultural force they represent is universal and thus transcends all particulars.

This principle is expressed in the impassioned poetry of Aeschylus, whose Prometheus Bound remains one of the clearest expositions to this day of the Christian power of agapic love which gives the heart the courage and the mind the self-discipline required to stand defiant against the tyrannical will of Zeus' law which posits that mankind remain as ignorant as the beasts, never to learn the secrets of the fire that is symbolic for his own creative potentiality.

It was this Promethean fire that burned in the heart of Augustine of Hippo as he arose to the stage of history and challenged the oligarchical priesthood of Rome that was trying desperately to sink a newly emerging

Christian world back into the pagan sophistry of empire. Its heat was felt again vividly in the person of Dante Alighieri who opposed the will of Venice when he revolutionized literature and the Italian language, creating the conditions for the later Italian Renaissance to blossom in the 15th century. In spite of the efforts of such Prometheans as Joan of Arc, King Louis the XI or Cardinal Mazarin and Jean Baptiste Colbert of France who led the 1648 Peace of Westphalia– the corruption wrought by Zeus in Europe had poisoned the culture too well for the fires to properly take hold. Amidst this demoralizing European decay of the 17th century, a new seat of fire abounding with ripe kindling was found an ocean away.

The seeds for humanity's rebirth appeared thus on the shores of a small colony known as New England, led by John Winthrop. This was the Winthrop who said during his inauguration of the Massachusetts Bay Colony in 1630; *"We shall be as a city upon a hill, the eyes of all people are upon us."*

Indeed the eyes of the world were upon them, as the hopes for a durable republican civilization dreamt of by Plato two millennia earlier could possibly finally take root. The early decades of this government bestowed with an independent charter founded explicitly upon the welfare of the governed, saw remarkable success. It had witnessed the issuance of the first colonial scrip to finance the industrial growth of the Sawguss Iron works and many internal improvements which led to a dramatic leap in the standards of living and cognitive powers of its people beyond anything seen in Europe. The cultural fire and taste for liberty grew fervently through this process and in spite of a desperate attempt on the part of Venetian puppets newly installed in England to stifle this fire in 1688, it continued to burn and the fight continued.

By the early 18th century, the leading Promethean in America who carried on John Winthrop's vision was a young disciple of Cotton Mather whose name was Benjamin Franklin.

Over the course of his entire life, this young man internalized the most universal lessons available to a creative mind and shaped himself patiently for a battle he knew was to come. Along the way, Franklin single-handedly sculpted a culture capable of internalizing and adding to the most profound ideas concerning man and nature then available.

Franklin's discovery of the principle of electricity shocked the world earning him the reputation among European humanists as the "Prometheus of America" who stole fire from the Gods and gave it to man. Most of the European elite were perplexed that a commoner from the land of barbarians on the outskirts of the Empire could possibly trump the greatest minds of Europe. What's more– they could not comprehend how Franklin's discovery of the universal principle of electricity was intertwined with his understanding of the universal principle of creative thought. After all, were one not made in the others' image, and if the microcosm (mind) not a reflection of the macrocosm (universe), then a discovery of principle such as he made, could never occur!

Most importantly, Franklin and his international co-thinkers of scientists, poets and statesmen also recognized that without *political freedom* those natural powers of creative reason which all humanity share in kinship and are the basis of our inalienable rights– can never be actualized. It is this essence of Natural Law which inspired Franklin to shape the leadership that later came to be known as the founding fathers of America.

The inability of all Zeus-minded elite to conceive of the unified relationship between moral and scientific law has always been the greatest blind spot of empire. History teaches us that any ruling power which believes it must crush freedom and creativity in the souls of those it wishes to rule in order to maintain what it perceives to be its self-interest, will always be self-doomed as the parasite which can only kill the host upon which its survival depends. Contemplating this phenomenon American poet Edgar Poe once famously stated; one may convince a bird that its nature is to creep and crawl like a worm, but that will only lead to a tortured and slow death since its nature has always been to soar.

The life's deeds and original writings of such keystone Protheans as Plato, Confucius, Augustine, Dante, Franklin et al remain invaluable resources for any who care to seek. Inversely, leading spokesman representing the oligarchical worldview also lived, acted and wrote their thoughts which are also widely available for any researcher (sadly more available than those writings of the aforementioned humanists).

But this only leaves one of our two questions answered. What about the second portion? What makes this version of Canada's "untold history" more truthful than anything else that came before it?

To begin with, no book on Canada that this author has ever encountered takes on the subject from the CONTEXT of universal history, and none have recognized that there can be no truthful history of Canada without taking into effect the dynamic of all world history as a battle of ideas.

I am convinced that it is by understanding this universal battle over ideas as it existed in Benjamin Franklin's mind, while observing his role in universal history, and his efforts to bring a young French colony named Quebec into this historical battle that the greatest insight into the paradox that is Canada can be gleamed.

When we observe that this dynamic of Universal history expressed by the Prometheus vs Zeus worldviews was at the heart of the American colonies' break from the British Empire, and as we identify this break as the single most important phenomenon of modern world history, then and only then, can a lawful understanding of Canada be grasped.

Just as our character in life is formed by the decisions we take (or fail to take) while we are alive, so too is the character of a nation formed. And by failing to accept the challenge of becoming the 14th colony to declare independence in 1776, a distorted anti-Promethean principle became implanted in our collective experience as a people in 1791, then again with the Act of Union of 1840, and again with the British North American Act of 1867 and yet again with the rise of "new nationalism" in 1963. While Promethean tendencies, being the natural state of humanity, have undoubtedly arisen from time to time in Canada's experience, it has too often occurred in a confused form. Never self-consciously as we have seen it manifest in such figures as Franklin, George Washington, Alexander Hamilton, William Gilpin, or Abraham Lincoln later.

While good Canadian intentions and creative efforts have contributed much prosperity and progress which we must cherish and celebrate, it must be recognized that more often than not, the inability of most Canadians, motivated by Promethean impulses, to reconcile those irreconcilable principles of monarchism and republicanism have led them to make tragic errors, thus undoing much of the good that they yearned to accomplish. This was clearly seen in the failed attempts by William Lyon Mackenzie and Louis Joseph Papineau to conduct their republican revolutions in 1837-38, in Sir Wilfred Laurier's attempts to create a customs union of the America's in 1911, Prime Minister William Mackenzie King's desires to construct a just post-war world and John Diefenbaker's failure to accomplish his Northern Vision in 1963.

When one begins to tune one's mind to looking at history from the standpoint of IDEAS of the future that should have been, rather than merely charting what came to pass as modern chroniclers are wont to do, may we then begin to explore history from a truthful standpoint.

# CHAPTER I – W.A.C. BENNETT: CANADA'S SPIRITUAL FATHER OF NORTHERN DEVELOPMENT

*"There's a great law of nature that goes something like this- what you don't use, you lose. If a person is a pianist and doesn't develop it, he loses his talent. If a person is a good pitcher and doesn't throw, he loses that talent. We are not going to sit by and watch potential development in British Columbia be held back by any source. Not big business, not by big labour, not by big government."*

*-B.C. Premier W.A.C. Bennett*

[Much of the pioneering research for this chapter was done by Robert Hux, Ph.D.]

The greatest opportunities to unleash progress and peace across the world exist today in the opening up the Arctic to development, and uniting Eurasia with the Americas by extending the China's New Silk Road (aka: One Belt One Road) through the Bering Strait which many are calling the North American Belt and Road Initiative (NABRI). A key element of the NABRI involves constructing the North American Water and Power Alliance (NAWAPA), advocated decades ago by the likes of John and Robert Kennedy.

It is tragic that such visionary thinking has been absent in our western culture for so long, that the belief that such initiatives were ever possible has been almost entirely crushed out of the hearts and minds of most citizens. The spirit of optimism of the Kennedy years has been abandoned. The challenges defined by John F. Kennedy for the American nation and to all those around the world who took personal pride in Mankind's space achievements must now be rekindled.

The majority of today's youth, and even fewer of today's baby boomers do not even believe that it is possible for mankind to exert any durable changes to nature which are not intrinsically destructive. It is the contention of this author that were our minds not severed from great Canadian endeavours, from even our recent past, through largely successful British supported attempts to re-write Canadian history, such pessimistic beliefs as we encounter today could not exist, and those powers of creative problem solving so essential for the survival of nations, could be nurtured anew. In short, with a proper understanding of the ideas of the past that gave birth to this dying present devoid of a future, a dark age, even at this late hour, were still avoidable.

It is for this reason that we will begin our report by introducing the reader to the vital story of William Cecil Bennett, the visionary Premier of British Columbia, admirer and sometimes collaborator of John F. Kennedy, who represented the tradition that a true Canadian patriot should aspire to achieve. Bennett's struggle for development directly intersects similar fights with allies in Ottawa such as Prime Minister John Diefenbaker, and groupings of leading figures around the Quiet Revolution in Quebec such as Premiers Jean Lesage and Daniel Johnson Sr. Internationally such networks in Canada were tied directly to those leading networks around President Charles De Gaulle of France, and President Kennedy's networks in the USA.

## A man with a purpose

A young man during the Great Depression, W.A.C. Bennett's recognition of the impotence of economic theories founded on ivory tower formulas, without grounding in reality, proved a vital insight that would serve him for the rest of his life. This insight would be the effect of watching formerly successful citizens living on the streets and begging for food, through no fault of their own. A commitment to heal those ills caused by human selfishness and folly would become a consuming passion which served him throughout a political career that would stretch for over thirty years in the British Columbia legislature, twenty of those as Premier. After having earned a living as a successful entrepreneur, Bennett would decide to make a move into politics as a Conservative Minister of the Legislative Assembly (MLA) in 1941, two years into Canada's involvement in World War II.

Bennett's first appointment involved his service as a member of the Post War Rehabilitation Council, whose mission was to prepare for the crisis which was waiting to occur as the flux of young soldiers returning from service would need to find productive employment and rebuild their lives. There was no way that the existent economy of British Columbia would be capable of handling such a flood of young men. The economy would have to be re-adjusted quickly to accommodate this vital need[1]. The council would produce two reports in 1943 and 1944, laying out a bold blueprint for uplifting peoples' productive capacities, which would soon become Bennett's lifelong devotion.

The blueprint would call for the vast development of British Columbia with a focus upon energy development, northern expansion, water management, agriculture, mining, forestry, rail construction, city building and of course, manufacturing. Industrial development to process as much raw material at home as possible was necessary in Bennett's mind in order to avoid falling into the age old trap, where one nation exports cheap resources for mere money while a dominant country maintains the vital industries, which perpetuates the backwardness of the raw material exporting nation. Such an imperial monetarist policy was the bane of the existence of the underdeveloped Dominion of Canada. Bennett refused to accept this practice. Among a vast spectrum of proposals, the council's plan called explicitly for developing the region of the Peace River in the north, the extension of rail lines deep into the north of the province and also the creation of a publicly owned hydroelectric authority to provide cheap electricity.

While attempts were being made to advance British Columbia's development in piecemeal fashion under the Liberal-Conservative coalition governments, the pace was too slow for Bennett's liking, and he found it necessary to leave the Conservative party in 1951 in order to temporarily become an independent MLA. He began organizing heavily to bring about the collapse of the coalition government through a vote of no confidence in

1952. During his time as an independent, Bennett saw a potential in re-organizing an underdog party known as Social Credit (Socred) that had never had more than a handful of seats at one time in B.C. However, using every ounce of his energy, Bennett organized outside of traditional party institutions to ensure that within several months, 19 seats would be won by Socred members.

While it is important to note that Social Credit would have its origins as a bizarre British run operation in the 1920s, the newly elected batch of Socred MLAs were almost entirely composed of regular working citizens. Barely a few hours of administrative experience could be found among any of the new representatives creating one of the most ideologically free cabinets in Canadian history.

Having 19 seats would be enough to win a provincial election, but not enough to earn the mandate necessary to push those large scale projects Bennett wanted. A second election was thus called nine months later, ensuring Socred a solid majority, and giving Bennett the flexibility to advance on various aspects of the blueprint all at once.

## Opening up the Great North

Unlike the small minded economists of today who, when confronted with the challenge of developing railroads across the Bering Strait, declare "but what is the point? There is no civilization there", Bennett was not subject to such short-sightedness. Taking the experiences of history seriously, Bennett understood that the first step to opening up new frontiers hinged upon developing advanced transportation systems, without which nothing could be done, and from which all would organically follow. A railroad is not the effect of civilization as "supply and demand" thinking would presume. Rather, civilization was the effect of the railroad.

It was understood by many at this time that British Columbia's natural potential was too vast to continue to go untouched and its population too concentrated to the south eastern corner of the province around Vancouver and Victoria. A 1942 U.S. survey of the area noted the problem in the following way; "If the northern part of the area has been held down in a vicious circle of under-development (scanty population, inadequate transportation routes, high cost of living, etc.) then it is entirely possible that the circle will have been cut by the provision of a vastly more adequate transportation system" [2]

The immediate problem that Bennett faced, was that the Pacific Great Eastern (PGE) was so mismanaged and undeveloped that not only did it merely service a small handful of lines touching the few population centers then in existence cusping the American border, but the provincial government had even tried desperately to sell it to both the federal government and Canada's two private transcontinental railways, but to no avail. Bennett went straight to work on the rehabilitation of the rail system and stated in 1954 "Of all the interests I have in public life, none is a greater challenge... no money in this province could pay me for the satisfaction I would feel if this railway were changed from a joke and put on a sound financial basis".

The rail and transport component of Bennett's plan would have two phases. The first phase would be from 1954-59 and the second from the mid-1960s to early 1970s. Throughout the 1950s, the PGE was extended to Dawson Creek, and Fort St. John in the Peace River district. Extensions across the south also abounded. After Ottawa continuously blocked his program and refused to participate in the financing of the operations, Bennett took on a more "go it alone stance", and continued to utilize the sovereign rights which Canadian provinces wield outside of federal jurisdiction to push forward with a second phase of rail extension in the 1960s and early 1970s[3] (See figure 2).

Throughout this process, Bennett's intentions to connect the rail lines deep into the Yukon, Alaska and the Great Slave Lake region of the Northwest Territories were transparent in countless speaking engagements. An illustration of the most likely Alaskan–Canadian rail lines promoted by Bennett can be seen in figure 3. To get there, connections had to be made from Fort St James to Takia Landing, and from Fort St John to Fort Nelson and onto Whitehorse. According to a 1968 study by Hedlin, Menzies and Associates Ltd, six routes in all were to be completed from British Columbia into the Yukon with additional routes stretching into the Northwest Territories, and Alaska.

As demonstrated in figure 2, these visionary plans were never fully completed, and limits to the PGE (now B.C. Rail) cut off at Takia Landing, Fort Nelson, and Dawson Creek without a single connection into the Arctic territories or Alaska. Tragically, due to the shift into post-industrial monetarism with the 1971 destruction of the Bretton Woods System, long term thinking has been so derailed that the rail line to Takia Landing has been made famous as the "mysterious rail to nowhere" which the government of British Columbia has up for sale for one dollar!

The Northern Vision program of a new John Diefenbaker leadership entering Ottawa in 1957 replacing a 22 year Liberal regime would vitalize Bennett. However due to the blowback by the powerful Ottawa mandarins occupying high level offices throughout Canada's Civil Service, Diefenbaker's Vision was aggressively subverted inducing a frustrated Bennett to comment in 1977: *"They talked northern vision, but produced none of it"* [4].

To what degree Bennett understood the highly coordinated subversion of Diefenbaker's "Northern Vision" from London's Foreign Office is not known. However, Bennett was in no way a naïve man, and his genius as a strategist would be unveiled during the years of the fight over British Columbia's water and energy resources [5].

# Bennett's Grand Design and its opposition

A core component in Bennett's Grand Design would be the building of hydroelectric stations to power the present and future industries and households of British Columbia, as well as provide for water management to the benefit of the USA and Canada. The potential for harnessing both was greater in no part of North America than in British Columbia, and the needs of a growing population would become dire if future oriented plans were not adopted immediately. To illustrate Bennett's sensitivity to the needs of the future, he would later write:

*"The greatest thing we need in our civilization, in our time, is not oil, not gas, but fresh water; not just any old water but fresh water. There's too little of it in the world. We're heading into a period of droughts. I am not prophesying doom, but we should be prepared... These people who are always criticizing dams don't know what they are talking about. We should be encouraging the building of dams everywhere in Canada. Of course, we shouldn't hurt our natural resources such as our fish. Of course, we should protect our natural beauty at the same time, but we should encourage dams to be constructed even for farmers on their ranches. If water flows through an area, build a dam! Governments should encourage that, because what is needed is an abundance of fresh water."[6]*

In advancing this component of his design, Bennett would be confronted with a coordinated backlash by the highest echelons of Britain's networks amongst the Canadian mandarins in Ottawa. The obstacles Bennett would have to overcome to advance this component of his development strategy would be enormous. The greatest were:

1)    The Ottawa controlled B.C. Electric company which refused to cooperate with his plan to develop the north.

2)    The Fight to subvert Diefenbaker's Northern Vision via a contraction of the money supply led by the Governor of the Bank of Canada, James Coyne

3)    The Davie Fulton– General Andrew McNaughton operation to break the American-Canadian program for the Columbia development in favour of a "Canada only" variant.

4)    The coordinated barrage of anti-Americanism in the media sponsored by leading British assets in Canada that had given birth to the strategy later dubbed Canada's "New Nationalism" and embodied in Pierre Elliot Trudeau's Just Society reform.

# A few words on continental development

The necessity of developing continental water management policies was first recognized in the late 19th century as the growing population of the western United States blossomed and Lincoln's Trans Continental Railway linked the two oceans for the first time. Canada's western population growth followed soon thereafter with the completion of the Canadian Pacific Rail from Montreal to Vancouver in 1885. The westerners of North America had found themselves trapped in territories that suffered massive water scarcity, while the great abundance of water resources in the unpopulated Canadian north went through its cycle essentially unused either by humans or even the biosphere. The first formal treaty signed between Canada and the USA to deal with this increasing need would be the Boundary Waters Treaty in 1909 which also established the International Joint Commission, although very little would come of it for the duration of the coming several decades.

By 1944, Prime Minister Mackenzie King and Franklin Roosevelt called upon the International Joint Commission (IJC) to accelerate programs that would mutually benefit both Countries with a focus upon the St. Lawrence Seaway on the east coast and the development of the Columbia River basin in the west. Though great strides had been made by networks of Quebec Premier Duplessis, Prime Minister St. Laurent and President Eisenhower to accomplish the St. Lawrence Seaway program by 1959, the long sought Columbia River development had made very little progress.

The importance of the Columbia River Basin was amplified by the fact that many of America's river systems along the Columbia River basin area were already dammed to near capacity (see figure 4.) and while great abundance had been achieved in agricultural and industrial output throughout the 1940s and 1950s, water and energy scarcity still loomed. Not only that, but the "Glacier dilemma" was creating a big problem for the Americans. The glaciers of the Canadian north are not at all unchanging, but rather partially melt in spring and refreeze in winter. This process creates a wide variance of the Columbia River's flow. The spring melt would result in floods every year wrecking havoc on agriculture, and the weak trickle in winter would make harnessing the full hydroelectric potential of the river impossible.

From 1940, American engineers had proposed a series of dams on the Canadian side that would act as catchments to store the water to regulate the flow, creating both flood controls in summer and a maximization of hydroelectricity production in winter. Plans were put forward by American engineers to build what was later to become known as the Mica, the Keenleyside and Duncan Dams on the Canadian side of the border while the Libby Dam was to be built on the American side. The Duncan and Libby dams would be located on the Kootenay River, which was a tributary of the Columbia. In exchange for the Canadian dams which would increase downstream benefits greatly, the American offer would make half of that newly created power available for British Columbia.

# A General Subversion

Plans to go through with these designs had been sabotaged largely by the subversive influence of anglophile war hero General Andrew McNaughton, Canadian chairman of the IJC from 1950-1962 [7] (see figure 5). McNaughton not only organized against the American designs, declaring any cooperation with America to be a move towards "continentalism" (and thus the loss of Canadian sovereignty), but he also favoured an alternative program which proposed to divert the Columbia and Kootenay rivers into the Fraser so that their flow would create power only for the Canadians and provide water supplies for the prairies, leaving the Americans out to hang. Had this program been accepted, then not only would the Columbia program as we know it not exist, but the great potential to construct NAWAPA would have been destroyed.

McNaughton would be among the powerful networks run by the Oxford Trained Mandarins of Ottawa's Civil Service who would attempt to destroy every continental approach to resource management presented during these years. Their favoured theme was the creation and exploitation of anti-American sentiments, and tapping into deep seated fears that

Figure 1. W.A.C Bennett, Premier of B.C., April 1955 in Ottawa. Library and Archives Canada, PA-115138. Photographer: Duncan Cameron

Figure 2. Building the Pacific Great Eastern Railway. John R. Wedley. B.C. Studies. no. 117, Spring 1998. p. 30

Figure 4. While most river systems along America's side of the Columbia River Basin were developed to capacity, the Canadian side was far behind. Here, the completed Columbia Dams.
wwww.nwd-wc.wsace.army.mil/report/colmap.htm

Figure 3. Proposed norhtern rail lines. John R. Wedley. B.C. Studies, no. 117, Spring 19988. pg. 44

Figure 5. Anglophile Gen. Andrew McNaughton. Library and Archives Canada

Canadians had of being annexed by the USA [8]. McNaughton's program provided a stubborn counterweight to the American government's unwilling-ness to pay for the high costs demanded of them by Ottawa for the system, and resulted in a stalemate that lasted years.

In order to get an idea of McNaughton's attitude and the effectiveness of the stalemate: the McNaughton Plan remained under discussion all the way until 1960, and when Premier Bennett decided to openly endorse the American proposal (after a drawn out battle with the Ottawa mandarins beginning in 1956), McNaughton attacked Bennett for allowing the Americans to *"walk into a house divided against itself and skin the occupants alive"*.

# Bennett's Two Rivers Policy breaks the stalemate

Previous to 1954, no possible resolution to the stalemate was forthcoming. Bennett, anxious for development, began demonstrating his creative powers to the great anxiety of Ottawa. At this time, Bennett began working with an American firm named Kaiser Corporation which had offered a plan to pay for the construction of a massive storage dam on Mica Creek and guaranteed that 20% of the power produced would be delivered to British Columbia. Bennett pushed for the Kaiser deal against massive backlash from all parties in the Provincial legislature. The federal government of Prime Minister St. Laurent, then fearing the loss of Ottawa's bargaining power on the Columbia, immediately responded by passing the International Rivers Improvement (IRI) Act of 1955. This act prohibited all parties from building improvements on an international river without federal license, thereby crushing the Kaiser deal. Taking this lesson to heart, Bennett resolved that no such manipulation by Ottawa would occur again.

A new opportunity to break the stalemate presented itself in 1957, when a prospecting survey conducted by the Swedish industrialist Axel Wenner-Gren in collaboration with Bennett had concluded that the Peace River in British Columbia's north held all of the requirements for a huge hydroelectric dam that would create the largest man-made reservoir in the world. The power from the Peace would not only be greater than the Columbia but could be delivered more cheaply. This discovery would become the origin of Bennett's Two River Strategy (see figure 6) and would provide one of the key bargaining chips to break the Ottawa-Washington stagnation.

Realizing the importance of this new bargaining chip, Bennett made the following elated statement at a press conference on October 8 1957:

*"This is the most momentous announcement I have ever made... the studies being conducted in the north indicated the feasibility of establishing in the Rocky Mountain Trench the greatest hydroelectric project in the world"* and would be *"entirely in the control of the government of British Columbia... this day is the most important that B.C. has experienced in its whole history. Surely now both Ottawa and the U.S. will realize we mean business."*

Bennett's program for the Peace would not impinge upon the 1955 IRI Act since the Peace River fell entirely within Canadian territory.

By early 1960, Bennett had openly begun organizing for America's Columbia River Treaty proposal which effectively put the nail in the coffin for the McNaughton Plan. An overjoyed Diefenbaker saw this as an opportunity to salvage his waning Northern Vision and immediate raced down to the USA to persuade President Eisenhower to sign a draft treaty (see figure 7) , which was then ratified in Ottawa and sent to Bennett. To everyone's surprise and bewilderment, Bennett did not sign. He was more committed to the Peace than anyone had hitherto imagined. No one could understand how anything could be made of that obscure, uninhabited region of the north. In the words of Bennett:

*"The criticism you had to listen to was terrible! First, they said you could never transmit power over that distance to Vancouver, the place where most of it would be needed and used. No, the distance was far too great! They had no vision. We stood alone against all the other parties, the federals, the other provincial governments, even the United States. They opted only for the Columbia; but we alone said that the Peace was vital for our province."[9]*

## More obstacles to disrupt the Peace

Using brilliant American System thinking, Bennett's entire plan for the Peace would hinge upon future productivity that had no existence in the present and yet would extinguish the debts incurred in the present and justify its construction. No present demand would justify the abundance of supply that would be delivered by the Peace, for that abundance was for the future. Bennett envisioned using the cash gained by selling Columbia River power to the Americans which would then pay for the building of a reservoir and hydro station on the Peace which in turn would provide the power for British Columbia's population and industry to flourish.

The first obstacle confronted by Bennett at this phase was to be found in the monetarist thinking that had dominated policy making in Canada at that time. The Two River Policy would nearly be destroyed when the Ottawa controlled power utility B.C. Electric that had a monopoly on all power distribution in the province, refused to agree to purchase power from the Peace citing the monetarist argument of "supply and demand". The monetarist reasoning would follow the following lines: "If the electricity from the Columbia provided from America to BC would more than meet the immediate demand for power in B.C., then no additional power generation would be needed, as none would be demanded... thus nothing should be built on the Peace." The fact that Columbia River proposals involved the Americans providing half of the newly generated hydro potential from its dams to Canadians meant that all possible demand would be satisfied, and anything greater (such as that which would be developed on the Peace) would be redundant.

A second obstacle which threatened to undermine the plan involved the intervention by the Federal Minister of Justice Davie Fulton who became Ottawa's chief spokesman and negotiator for the Columbia. Fulton had been an advocate of the McNaughton Plan and critic of the Two River Policy. He and a group of young Oxford trained Rhodes scholars known as "Fulton's Boys" would establish a faction within the Diefenbaker cabinet that worked tirelessly against all attempts by Diefenbaker and his closest collaborators to apply nation building policies into action. Two of Fulton's Boys, Michael Pitfield and Marc Lalonde would later on lead Trudeau's close inner circle of advisors.

A third obstacle was found in the absence of financial aid from Ottawa. This lack of financial support was the direct effect of the Bank of Canada's money contracting policy during 1957-1960. The effect of the money contraction would lead to a long public fight between the bank's Governor, James Coyne and Prime Minister Diefenbaker whose Northern Vision was handicapped when credit was intentionally dried up. The fight led to Diefenbaker's firing of the Bank of Canada's Governor James Coyne in July 1961, an action that began the process that ultimately led to the defeat of Diefenbaker's government in 1963.[10]

Up through May 1961, Fulton and Coyne's intrigues resulted in an Ottawa policy that castrated Diefenbaker and posed unworkable conditions upon Bennett. Ottawa objected to Bennett's desire to sell downstream benefits to the Americans and demanded that instead of cash, British Columbia receive only electricity from the USA's newly maximized hydro potential. Obviously, Bennett was furious, seeing as how the cash was necessary to build the Peace River, and the excess electricity provided from the downstream power generating stations would have been far more than an under developed British Columbia could use. To make matters worse, Ottawa demanded joint federal–provincial control over the Columbia River projects in return for any monetary aid. Having proven its perpetual intention to sabotage provincial development, Bennett found this joint control to be entirely unacceptable.

The primary argument Fulton used against Bennett's program would be built on a fallacy which Bennett would frequently attack for years. Where Ottawa asserted that once the treaty was signed to sell power back to the Americans, it could never be reversed, and that power would be forever lost from Canada, Bennett would constantly point out that his program called for a treaty of sixty years broken into two instalments, whereby the second instalment would contractually oblige the USA to return B.C.'s share of power in the form of electricity or cash. Bennett would describe the deal and his battle with his critics thus:

*"Now critics say it didn't pay for all the cost of the dams, this cash we received from the Americans. It was a sell-out to the Yankees, they say. The answer to that accusation is that of all the treaties ever concluded between Canada and a foreign country, this one was the best for British Columbia and for Canada. The critics could only see the first half of the treaty but the agreement covers sixty years, not thirty. We were only paid for the first half... How stupid these people are. They always forget about the last half of the treaty when the United States must give back to us at our border our share of the power, our rightful half. Whatever they've developed over thirty years, half of it comes back in either power or in cash."[11]*

Bennett would deal with these obstacles not by playing within the closed system thinking demanded by the conditions set forth by the Ottawa mandarins and their British controllers. Instead, Bennett would apply his powers of the creative flank and throw over the entire chess board at every opportunity. In this case, he would seek the help of John F. Kennedy and take over B.C. Electric.

# Bennett's Flank

On November 1961, in order to gain additional political support in his battle with Fulton, Bennett flew down to Seattle, Washington to attend a memorial for Senator Warren Magnusen's 25 years of service. The real reason for his attendance is to be looked for in the long closed door meeting he had with fellow attendee, President John F. Kennedy. Meetings between U.S. Presidents and provincial Premiers are relatively unprecedented and the meeting between Kennedy and Bennett created a diplomatic incident. While no official transcript of the meeting exists, the results could be felt when five days later, Kennedy's Secretary of the Interior, Stewart Udall, loudly denounced Fulton's opposition to Bennett's grand plan as "stuff and nonsense".

An enraged Fulton flew immediately to Victoria, B.C. to confront the Premier. Bennett, though having been seen just minutes earlier, could not be found to greet him, leaving a dejected Fulton to hop back on the plane and return to Ottawa. The decision by Kennedy to support Bennett's Two Rivers policy over that of Ottawa's version of the treaty would contribute to a deep rift between Diefenbaker and Kennedy that would unfortunately last throughout the duration of Kennedy's short life.

The final obstacle that had to be dealt with was the lack of cooperation from B.C. Electric to provide contracts to B.C. Peace River Power Development Company created by Axel Wenner-Gren, of which B.C. Electric was a large shareholder. Contracts to purchase the power were absolutely necessary in order to begin construction on the Peace River. Frustrated by months of inaction, Bennett arranged a meeting with the head of B.C. Electric at a hotel in London. Having asked why it was that B.C. Electric was not cooperating with the needs of the province, Bennett was informed that the problem resided in Ottawa's direct control over the utility which had no intention of permitting the Peace to go forward. Bennett laid out his ultimatum in the following way:

*"There's a great law of nature that goes something like this- what you don't use, you lose. If a person is a pianist and doesn't develop it, he loses his talent. If a person is a good pitcher and doesn't throw, he loses that talent. We are not going to sit by and watch potential development in British Columbia be held back by any source. Not big business, not by big labour, not by big government. I want you to clearly understand that. I will give you reasonable time, but it will be short."[12]*

Within several months, after no change in the utility's stance occurred, Bennett introduced Bill 5, also known as the Power Development Act into the provincial legislature offering $180 million for the acquisition not only of Wenner-Gren's Peace River Power Development Company, but the entire B.C. Electric from its owner, the federally controlled B.C. Power Corporation. This was now August 1961, and after a short legal battle, the sum paid for the takeover was $197 million to cover interest and legal fees.

Since British Columbia now owned the utility that would build and operate all the dams on the Canadian side of the Columbia, Bennett could uniquely set the treaty terms. This would be the birth of B.C. Hydro, and the construction of the Two River Plan.

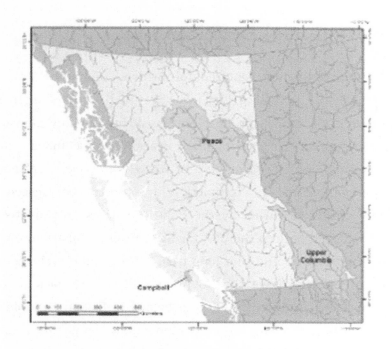

Figure 6 above: The Two River Policy would call for
the harnessing of both the Columbia and Peace River basins
pacificclimate.org/project/hydrologic-modelling-peace-campbell-
and-columbia-river-watersheds

Below: Eisenhauer and Diefenbaker sign the Columbia River Treaty
Jan. 17, 1961, Photo United States Government

# Interprovincial Development

With the terms Bennett required for British Columbia's Two Rivers Policy established, a final treaty was ratified with Bennett's full satisfaction in 1964 by Lester Pearson, President Lyndon Johnson and himself (see figure 8). The success of the Peace River was made evident to all once it began supplying over 90% of B.C. Hydro's electrical power to British Columbia after its completion in 1968. The agreed upon hydroelectric output produced by the Columbia dams (completed from 1967-1972) was sold back to the USA for $254 million dollars in one lump sum for the first half of a 60 year long treaty. The second cycle, scheduled to end by 2024 would have the US provide electricity back to Canada instead of cash. $64 million would be provided to British Columbia from the U.S. as compensation for the operation of the dams that minimized flood damages in the U.S.

The immediate revenue of this deal mixed with the increased productivity and industrial activity effected by the construction of the Peace River resulted in Bennett's ability to invest into various social programs such as universal medical coverage, and wide public improvements. To top it off, $100 million loan was also provided to Quebec's Premier Jean Lesage who had encountered similar problems as Bennett had with Ottawa's Civil Service and yet yearned to continue developing the hydroelectric and transportation programs begun by the Duplessis leadership of l'Union Nationale that came before him.

Like the case of Quebec's hydroelectric potential in the north of the province, British Columbia had encountered many naysayers that said transmitting electricity across the long distances separating the Peace River from most populated centers in the province was impossible, as the electrical power loss due to the heating of the wires would be too great. The discoveries which had to be made to allow for the transmission of electrical power at much higher voltages and correspondingly lower current flows lead to British Columbia's and Quebec's engineers becoming world innovators in the field of electrical transmission.

# An Introduction to the Provincial Fight to Develop

It is appropriate at this stage of our report to address the vital role played by two types of conferences that had occurred to make the development of British Columbia and other provinces possible. With the tightly controlled federal government that is itself greatly influenced by the British run Civil Service, and highly fragmented provincial system, the path of Canada's development has taken an unlikely, yet necessary route. This development had occurred generally in spite of, and rarely through any help of, the Federal Government, with nation building Premiers often being forced to lead Ottawa by the nose in advancing great works. (See appendix)

The mechanism most often selected through the 1950s and 1960s to set the conceptual framework for visionary ideas, so often lacking from Ottawa, and that crossed beyond provincial and national borders involved a variety of conferences in which leading state, provincial, and private sector leaders, desiring development would network and strategize for their own and the country's benefit.

The first and most common events were the Interprovincial Conferences which addressed a variety of issues from local concerns, to large scale agricultural, and resource management. These conferences would facilitate such deals as the $100 million aid and technical expertise provided from

Bennett to Quebec's Jean Lesage in 1964. The second type of conference on the west coast was known as the Alaska-British Columbia- Yukon conferences (A-BC-Y), of which three had formally occurred between 1960 and 1964. A brief examination of the contents of these conferences shall provide the reader a wonderful glimpse into the strategic thinking and possibilities which were coming into existence during this vital period of history.

## Learning the A-BC-Ys

*"We think that this is the time- and timing is important- and this is the place for the new frontier and the northern vision; because if ever there was a place that needed planned growth and millions of dollars in expenditure, it is northern B.C., the Yukon and Alaska... The time for action is now, not ten years from now! Last week the Russian ambassador told me in a very clear way, that in the part of Russia opposite us, Russia is spending 40 percent of all its capital expenditures. We in the U.S. and Canada cannot sit idly by and see that great economic development take place without matching it with more than words"*

These were the opening remarks made by Premier Bennett at the second A-BC-Y Conference in Juno Alaska in 1960 [13]. The three conferences that would occur amongst Alaska, British Columbia and the Yukon between 1960 and 1964 contained the germ seeds of the greater continental cooperation that was being organized as early as 1870. While intercontinental visions had begun with the planned linking of telegraph wires through the Bering Strait as early as the Alaska purchase of 1867, and the 1905 designs for a rail tunnel connecting America to Russia through Canada [14], the First World War and speculative economic insanity of the 1920s had kept such visions from being realized.

The needs of World War II would kick start the orientation to joint cooperative development in the north beginning with the formation of the U.S.-Canadian Joint Economic Committee (USCJEC) in January 1943. The Canada Air routes to Alaska and Yukon, the Alaska Highway, and a pipeline and refinery system known to provide aviation fuel for the Northwest Staging System also known as the Canol Project would begin during this time. A 1943 New York Times editorial on the USCJEC would read "The cooperative project outlined may foreshadow a new kind of relationship, and one that may be imitated elsewhere on the globe. Economic areas do not always run with political areas. Friendly adjoining governments may be able to overcome this difficulty, to the general advantage. Political Boundaries may simply become less important." This motion towards continental development should not be confused with the contemporary monetarist atrocity of the North American Free Trade Agreement (NAFTA).

While the momentum to advance continental programs was largely dissipated after World War II, Bennett would revive the spirit alongside like minded thinkers such as Alaskan Governor William Egan. After two important meetings between Bennett and the Alaskan Territorial Governor in 1954 and 1956, the A–BC–Y Conferences would be formed in order to help advance the construction of the PGE Rail into Alaska via a variety of routes, as well as provide hydroelectric power to the Alaskan Panhandle. The panhandle is an area devoid of hydroelectric potential, yet strategically rich in resources, and Pacific ports [15]. Due to the destructive role of Ottawa and Gen. McNaughton at the IJC, the third and final A–BC–Y conference in 1964 emphasized that further U.S.-Canada joint development of hydropower should proceed outside of the control of the IJC[16]. It is known that NAWAPA was discussed at the third conference, but as the reports would not made public, it cannot yet be reported in what way it was received or presented.

NAWAPA's design was begun in 1954 and, after one of its lead engineers had been hired by the Ralph M. Parsons Company in 1958, its development had become the company's policy. By Spring 1964, a U.S. Senate Subcommittee on Western Water development, led by Senator Frank Moss, was formed in order to conduct a comprehensive evaluation of NAWAPA. Their report, published in October of that year, found that since NAWAPA would store and deliver a much greater amount of water with significantly fewer projects (dams, canals, tunnels, etc.) than would be possible even through the construction of all the projects which had been studied or authorized by U.S. federal or non-federal agencies, a full engineering feasibility study was warranted (see figure 9).

As two key bottlenecks for the water's journey into southern Canada and USA were the Peace River and Columbia, it is safe to say that the final conception of the NAWAPA design was given its modern form through Bennett's initiatives on the Columbia River Treaty.

It is undoubtedly the case that leading engineering and pro-development networks across North America would have been very familiar with the program before its official unveiling. What Bennett's view of NAWAPA is has not yet been revealed to the authors of this report, however based upon a Canadian Broadcasting Corporation (CBC) interview from 1961 Bennett's view regarding river systems and water exports integral to the NAWAPA design were transparent:

*"We have in British Columbia four great river systems, and we have the greatest potential hydroelectric development of any part of the whole continent. And we're not to be compared to other parts of Canada, where they haven't got this great abundance of potential hydroelectric power. We have the Columbia River. We have the Fraser River. We have the Peace River. We have the Liard River. We have the Taku. We have the Yuka, and many many other rivers. In fact, a total of a potential of 40 million horsepower [30 gigawatts]. And we have a great asset,*

*which is now being exported, unused, for which we do not receive a single nickel. It's exported out to the oceans. The Arctic Ocean, and the Pacific Ocean unused. We are not doing a good job regarding this great natural resource".*

To avoid venturing into speculative territory, choosing to remain instead on firm ground, we can say that the majority of those water systems outlined by Bennett in this interview have major roles to play in the NAWAPA design. Necessary support components to NAWAPA's construction would have necessitated massive rail development and industrial potential across Northern B.C. and into the Yukon and Alaska reflected in the rail extension strategy begun by Bennett in 1954. Holding in ones' mind the fact of Bennett's intended Alaska- B.C. rail connection, and other uncompleted rail extensions outlined above, as well as the hydroelectric generation on the Fraser which he was fighting to develop when he was defeated in the 1972 B.C. election, we must conclude that all of the organic ingredients for NAWAPA's development were on hand under Bennett's visionary leadership and very present during the proceedings of each of the A–BC–Y Conferences.

# The 1963 Paradigm Shift: The Dream Fades

Everyone participating in these conferences could sense that the world was quickly changing for the worse. JFK's assassination opened the gates for the unleashing of the Vietnam war, a wave of traumatic political assassinations of great leaders struck with lightning speed, and a slide into cultural irrationalism with the emergence of the sex–rock–drugs counterculture paradigm was draining the life from Bennett's vision. The time for such visionary programs was quickly running out.

Figure 8. Johnson, Bennett and Pearson ratify
the Columbia River Treaty on Sept. 16, 1964

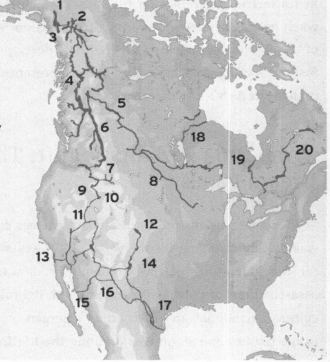

# REGIONAL
## BREAKDOWN

1. Susitna Reservoir
2. Yukon Reservoir
3. Copper Reservoir
4. Taku Lift
5. Canadian/Great-Lakes Waterway
6. Rocky Mountain Trench
7. Sawtooth Lifts
8. Dakota Waterway
9. Sawtooth Tunnel
10. Great Basin Waterway
11. Lake Nevada
12. Colorado Reservoir
13. Baja Aqueduct
14. Colorado Aqueduct
15. Sonora Aqueduct
16. Chihuahua Aqueduct
17. Rio-Grande Aqueduct
18. Hudson Bay Seaway
19. James Bay Seaway
20. Knob Lake Barge Canal

Figure 9. NAWAPA will use the topographic and climatological features of the North
American continent to collect and store excess water from rivers in Alaska, Yukon Territory,
and B.C. for distribution to water deficient areas of Canada, U.S. and northern Mexico. Also,
exces runoff of northward flowing rivers will be used to increase the water supply for the
prairies and the Great Lakes.                                    www.larouchepac.com

The recently created cult of "environmentalism" was serving as a new religion for a disenchanted youth generation trained to blame all of the imperialistic folly of the postwar world, not on the oligarchical system that was taking over society, but rather on the nuclear family, Christianity, and the belief that scientific and technological progress could support a continuously growing population. It seemed that planning for the future needs was not as important as "squares" like Bennett thought, as youth across North America and Europe seemed to "discover" all on their own, that humanity was not something worth saving after all.

The anti-science, anti-technological growth green policy would be cultivated by British agents within the Canadian and American establishments not to save nature, but rather to desperately put blockades on the continuation of programs such as the Bennett Grand Design. The first such program was the creation of the Aitlin Lakes Provincial Park to forestall the hydro plans for the Yukon River [17]. To this would later be added the first wave of conservation lands sponsored by the Canadian government under Prime Minister Pierre Trudeau and the $4.5 million dollar grants supplied to the Nature Trust of B.C. that would remove British Columbia territories vital to continental development from consideration [18]. These programs would be established specifically to halt the construction of the NAWAPA design.

The abolishment of large scale programs that inspire the imagination of citizens to leap outside of a closed framework of local concerns is today and has always been the preeminent drive of the oligarchical system. No society under any form of government, which is properly awakened to the greater needs and potential of the future can be stopped from pursuing a mission that is in line with creative reason. This also means that since oligarchical systems such as that embodied by today's British Empire can only maintain their existence when a population is kept small minded and fearful of change, such projects which awaken a spirit of creative change and improving nature as well as civilization are the greatest threat to empire.

Those programs advanced by the likes W.A.C. Bennett, Diefenbaker, Lesage and Daniel Johnson Sr. have now become the inspiration of fear and hatred from many such Canadians that have been victimized by several generations of misanthropic propaganda wearing the mask of patriotism.

# Bringing Bennett's Dream Back to Life

Lyndon LaRouche's policies for a New Bretton Woods and Glass-Steagall would provide Canada with the tools to begin to quickly return to the paradigm of creative change, and future planning last actively embodied by the likes of Bennett and his international collaborators. If the choice were made to defend human life at all cost and without any compromise from the emerging dark age which is fast creeping upon civilization, then programs such as NAWAPA, and the Bering Strait Tunnel would be the natural continuation of programs already begun decades ago, and expressed by Bennett's Grand Design, JFK's Apollo mission, and Diefenbaker's Northern Vision. Combined with joint collaborative programs with China and Russia on Arctic development and Asteroid Defense, the future could become very bright indeed.

# Bibliography

- David J. Mitchell, *W.A.C. Bennett and the Rise of British Columbia*, With a New Afterword, Douglas & McIntyre, Vancouver/Toronto, 1995.

- Roger Keene and David C. Humphreys, *Conversations with W.A.C.Bennett*, Methuen Press, Toronto, 1980.

- Neil A. Swainson, Conflict over the Columbia, *The Canadian Background to an Historic Treaty, Canadian Public Administration Series*, the Institute of Public Administration of Canada, McGill-QueensUniversity Press, Montreal, 1979.

- British Columbia, Ministry of Energy, Mines, and Petroleum Resources, *History of the Columbia River Treaty*.

- John R. Wedley, *A Development Tool: W.A.C.Bennett and the PGE Railway*, BC  Studies, no. 117, Spring 1998, pp. 29–50.

- P.R. Johannson, *A Regional Strategy: the Alaska-British Columbia-Yukon Conferences*, BC Studies, no.28, Winter 1975–76, pp. 29–52.

- Daniel Macfarlane, *The Value of a "Coyne": The Diefenbaker Government and the 1961 Coyne Affair*, University of Ottawa, 2008.

- Peter C. Newman, *Renegade in Power: The Diefenbaker Years*, McClelland and Stewart Ltd., 1963.

# CHAPTER II - JOHN DIEFENBAKER AND THE SABOTAGE OF THE NORTHERN VISION

*"We intend to launch for the future, we have laid the foundations now, the long range objectives of this party. We ask from you a mandate; a new and a stronger mandate, to pursue the planning and to carry to fruition our new national development programme for Canada. .. This national development policy will create a new sense of national purpose and national destiny."*

-John Diefenbaker, Prime Minister of Canada (1957-1963)

The years following World War II featured the greatest boom in economic progress and quality of life ever experienced in history. Today, the reasons for this acceleration of development of Canada as well as much of the world are largely misdiagnosed by historians and economists who, consciously or not, know nothing of the principled struggle between the American and British Systems and are totally ignorant of basic elementary principles of physical economy.

Previous knowledge of these dynamics was understood clearly by those few who, for good or for ill, have inflected the curvature of universal history, and without such knowledge quickly regained, no hope exists for our current population and its organic leadership to escape the tragic devolution of cultural, economic and intellectual life now pressing upon our future.

The present paper intends to shed light on the sometimes very paradoxical dynamics surrounding the failed Northern Vision and National Development Policy of Canada's 13th Prime Minister John G. Diefenbaker who led the Conservative Party to its first victory in 22 years in 1957 and remained in power until 1963. The broad scope of his Northern Vision policy would not be permitted to unfold for reasons that none but key officials in London working through Canada's Privy Council Office and Civil Service would truly know anything about.

While a fuller presentation of those years preceding Diefenbaker shall be left for another report, it is important, here and now, to run through certain key dynamics which shaped the world in which John Diefenbaker was entering when he was elected for a second term as an MP for Lake Centre, Saskatchewan in 1945.

# Post-War Visions Clash

The years 1945-1957 would be pregnant with seeds of potential as Franklin Roosevelt's post war vision elaborated in his "Four Freedoms" would nearly become manifest across the world. British colonialism was considered an obsolete relic of the Victorian epoch whose time had finally passed

It was during this period that the optimistic recognition of humanity's true mission would begin to penetrate to the forefront of general popular understanding. This would be the understanding that human nature was not located within the narrow confines of "limited resources" to be balanced and distributed during a given "state of existence" governed by entropic laws of "diminishing returns" in time and space. Instead, human nature's true purpose was to be located in the future potential that could be created by breaking out of the boundary conditions imposed by finite resources and leaping to new platforms of scientific and technological development.

With the nuclear age and the frontiers of space quickly opening up to humanity's sphere of influence, no fixed end point to this progress was assumed by the major part of populations of the world. Could it be that a new hope would finally be realized after centuries of oligarchical suppression?

Alas, another dynamic was pressing against this potential. The reaction of a wounded British Empire would be expressed most vividly in the anti-thesis to Roosevelt's Vision embodied in Winston Churchill's nightmarish defense of Empire. After Roosevelt's untimely death in 1945, Sir Winston Churchill would lay out the Empire's vision for the post war world beginning with the dropping of atomic bombs on a ready to surrender Japan followed by an Anglo-American alliance organized by a new financial (and often military) re-colonization to be set into motion through Churchill's Wall Street lackey President Harry S Truman [1]. This process would be amplified by Churchill's infamous 1946 "Iron Curtain" speech in Fulton Missouri, which would usher in the new bipolar age of the Cold War. This new era of geopolitics would begin by inducing former allies to become bitter enemies. In this new world dis-order, the red terror, McCarthyism, and the perpetual fear of nuclear annihilation would organize the culture and geopolitical relationships of all nations, and bring about an absolute schism of nations between the "democratic-capitalist" ideology on the one side and "communist-marxist" ideology on the other. The painful weight of this un-natural schism would shape the unfolding mentalities and policies for the coming decades.

As it would later be revealed, the controlling hand of both the Communist International, as well as western European and American military doctrines throughout the Cold War would always be found in London, evidenced by the likes of MI6's triple agent Kim Philby, the Socialist Fabians of the London School of Economics, Chatham House's Royal Institute for International Affairs and Bertrand Russell's International Institute for Applied Systems Analysis. The latter organization would spread its tentacles throughout MIT, Harvard, the Rand Corporation, and Soviet policy making circles alike. These British Empire networks would lead the call for "World Government" demanding the replacement of the sovereign nation-state system with a one world bureaucracy of "enlightened dictators" enforcing their will through the supranational military apparatus of NATO. Their thinking would be founded upon a radical positivist outlook called "systems analysis", and "information theory" which would attempt to lock all branches of human knowledge into its cage.

Within this dynamic that found the world often sitting precariously close to nuclear annihilation and death, the pulsing thirst for creativity and life would find various means of expression through different leaders from different cultures the world over, united by a common commitment to natural law, and unbounded progress.

# The Power and Downfall of C.D. Howe

The realization of Canada's potential for growth under the Liberal Party of Prime Minister Mackenzie King would not have occurred except for the brilliant manoeuvring of key strategists such as his "Minister of Everything" C.D. Howe and a small grouping of like-minded thinkers, who in various degrees comprehended the anti-human influence of the British Empire within Canada that longed for stagnation and control. Were it not for the collaboration of key leaders in American industry and politics with groups of their Canadian counterparts, it can almost be guaranteed that the stunning growth rates of the Canadian physical economy seen during these post war years would never have been
permitted to occur.

The driving force behind the Liberal Party's success during this period would be the American trained engineer turned politician Clarence Decatur Howe who remained the guiding force behind both PM Mackenzie King and his replacement Louis St. Laurent from 1935 to 1957. C.D. Howe's admiration of Franklin Delano Roosevelt would not only help re-organize Canada's industry during the war, but would provide the political economic solution for Howe in ushering in a wave of large scale projects that would define an unstoppable potential for growth, and overthrow the closed system thinking built into the structure of the Canadian political system and its imperial constitution of 1867.

Such game changing programs included the construction of the St. Lawrence Seaway, the Avro Arrow program, the Canadian Deuterium Uranium reactor (CANDU) technology, the Trans-Canada Highway, large scale rail, pipelines, mining and vast new heavy industries. Such programs would increase the Canada–USA exports from 42% in 1939 to 60% in 1955, and imports from 66% in 1939 to 73% in 1955 [2]. Purchasing power would increase by a factor of three over this period. The three means which C.D. Howe would use to advance Canada's development during these years would be:

1) The cheap credit provided via loans through the Bank of Canada (nationalized by Mackenzie King in 1937),

2) The investment capital of enthusiastic American enterprise and boosts in trade with America [3], and

3) The sweeping legal powers granted to him via the invoking of the War Measures Act of World War II and extended during the Korean War.

The War Measures Act would permit a Government of Canada, for the first time in history, to bypass bureaucratic red tape and parliamentary "party politics" for the sake of the development of the nation and the General Welfare. The incredible fact that C.D Howe would manage to use these broad powers long after WW II had come to an end is worthy of a study in and of itself, yet it would be these same broad war powers that would also contribute to the Liberal Party's downfall in June 1957 under the populist accusations that C.D. Howe was a dictator who disdained parliamentary politics. As far as the second part of the accusation was concerned, it was absolutely true, yet not for the superficial reasons that

Left:
Canada's "Minister of Everything" (1937–1957) C.D. Howe

Above: C.D. Howe inspecting a lens with a Canadian scientist

Right:
Sir Esme Howard, Prime Minister William Lyon Mackenzie King, and Round table controller Vincent Massey at the Canadian Legation during a visit to Washington on Nov. 22, 1927

Below:
John F. Kennedy and Dwight D. Eisenhauer

his accusers intended.

These accusations were amplified during a 1956–57 fight to build the largest pipeline in Canadian history bringing oil from Alberta to Quebec, providing an $80 million federal loan to American contractors to facilitate the process. The resistance in Parliament to the loan was absolute and condemnation of "selling Canada off to the Yankees" echoed throughout the corridors of Ottawa and reverberated deeply in the population through the press.

When C.D. Howe unwisely introduced a bill in parliament which would eliminate the expiration date of his war powers and then repeatedly called for "closure" of Parliament in order to shut down any attempts to contest the pipeline resolution, all hell effectively broke loose. As necessary as such actions may have been at the time, his enemies took the opportunity to stoke the flames of anti-Liberal (and anti-American) sentiment throughout the population. Little beknownst to C.D. Howe, these flames had been carefully lit and fueled by arsonists years before.

## The Rise of the CIIA's "New Nationalism"

When John Diefenbaker would take power in 1957, overthrowing the 22 year reign of the Liberal Party, the flames of anti-Americanism were becoming a raging furnace. This heated sentiment was the product of a strategy instituted by leading British operatives working within the umbrella group of the Canadian Institute for International Affairs (CIIA) to induce an artificial fear of America.

The CIIA would be Canadian version of Britain's Royal Institute for International Affairs (aka: Chatham House) founded in 1921 with similar

IIA branches throughout the Commonwealth. The CIIA had been formed in 1928 as a new incarnation of the Canadian Roundtable and would promote the Empire's post World War I strategy of dismantling sovereign nation-states using the mechanism of the League of Nations. After the failure of the League in 1940, the CIIA would enforce the new strategy of perverting the United Nations and organize for World Government under new supranational military, banking and regulatory structures.

The first of the two most influential CIIA run Royal Commissions whose design was to reshape Canada for this purpose, was the 1952 Massey Commission report on American infiltration of the Canadian Culture. The report of the Royal Commission on National Development in the Arts, Letters and Sciences would list prescriptive "remedies" to cure Canadian culture of its American influences in media, education and the arts, most of which would be adopted soon thereafter to shape a new synthetic Canadian culture. Among the variety of influential positions help by Vincent Massey would be privy councilor, Governor General (1952-59), High Commissioner to London (1935-46) and leader of the Roundtable Group in Canada. Massey's counterpart in the Roundtable Movement would be CIIA Honorary Secretary George Parkin de Glazebrooke, head of the Canadian New Joint Services Intelligence Agency which functioned as a Central Intelligence Agency of Canada. Massey himself would serve as vice-president of the CIIA.

The second piece of CIIA sponsored piece of anti-American conditioning would surface during this period in the form of the explosive 1957 Royal Commission report on Economic Prospects for Canada. This sister report was designed to make the case that were Canada not to break away from the vast American investment and economic influence that had developed under the post war Liberal Party, then the loss of sovereignty and absorption into the "American Empire" was inevitable.

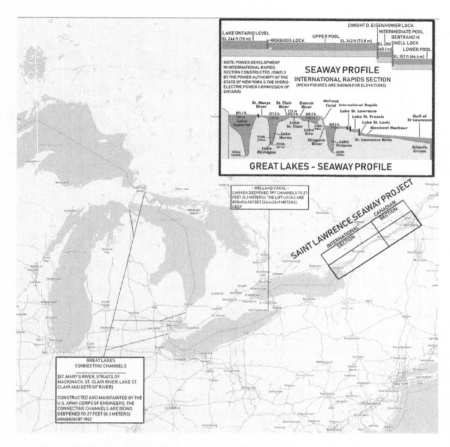

Under C.D. Howe's 20 year leadership, some of Canada's greatest national projects were completed- including the St. Laurence Seaway (above) and the Trans-Canada highway featured in red at left.
Other major projects featured on the next page: Avro Arrow (the world's first supersonic jet), and Canada's nuclear industry

**Above:** An artist's rendition of Canada's Avro Arrow supersonic jet. Unfortunately all working planes were cut down for scrap metal leaving only broken hearts and lost potential as Canada's finest aerospace engieers left for NASA

**Below:** Aerial photo of the Bruce Nuclear Generating Station near Kincardine Ontario. Photo by Chuck Szmurlo taken March 15, 2006. Canada's nuclear industry was built under the guidance of Howe.

The Commission was popularly known as the Gordon Commission, after its chairman Walter Lockhart Gordon who also served as chair of the National Executive Committee of the CIIA while also heading Canada's largest accounting firm and management consulting company. Other significant figures on the Commission would be Rhodes Scholar A.E. Grauer and Maurice Lamontagne. Lamontagne would rise to prominence as an enemy of Duplessis' Union National in Quebec and soon become President of the Privy Council (1964-65). Grauer would serve as president of B.C. Electric and its holding company B.C. Powercorp and would soon be locked in a battle with B.C. Premier W.A.C. Bennett over the development of the Peace River in northern B.C. [4].

As the later battles of Dwight Eisenhower and John F. Kennedy against the British Empire's Wall Street axis would prove, at this time, America's character as an imperialist nation was not at all determined [5]. In fact, what the masters of the CIIA centered in London's RIIA/Chatham House truly feared was that Canada would finally become a sovereign national republic as so many countries were choosing to become throughout the world at this time, under the influence of the United States' leadership political and economic leadership. Canada's proximity to the British Empire's historic nemesis, and vital geographical position between the Soviets and Americans, made the threat of losing this valuable geopolitical territory that much greater, especially as the population of Canada was becoming so prosperous specifically due to their collaboration with the Americans.

The anti-American rhetoric that Diefenbaker would popularly use during his bid for the leadership of Canada must be understood as having occurred within a context heavily shaped by the above factors influencing it. As events would later go on to demonstrate, this anti-American, nationalistic image created by Diefenbaker was selected as a populist means of attaining political power. Diefenbaker's choice to rise to power on the tide of populist sentiment would later contribute to his own downfall.

## The Profile of a Tragic Personality

Before proceeding to the substance of the Diefenbaker program, a brief note on his personality is in order.

John Diefenbaker would have the misfortune of being both a devout believer in human progress on the one side, while also a believer in the greatness of the British Empire on the other. In his memoirs Diefenbaker would write:

*"I am a Canadian, first, last and always, and to me the monarchy remains a vital force in the Canadian constitution. Not only is it the cornerstone of our institutional life, it remains a highly functional and necessary office... More important are the prerogative powers of the monarch to be consulted, to advise and to warn on all matters of state. The Queen, these twenty four years after her accession to the throne, is perhaps the most knowledgeable person in the world in the fields of Commonwealth and foreign affairs. As Prime Minister, I benefited from her wisdom."*

How an admirer of Abraham Lincoln and defender of progress could hold such views is paradoxical but not incomprehensible. This personality flaw is an important theme amongst many Anglo Saxon Commonwealth policy makers and is a simple effect of the naïve belief in a British revisionist history which has falsely attributed every advance of civilization and democracy to the "beneficent fruits of Imperialism". In actual fact, contrary to British revisionist history, progress, democracy and the increase of the powers of productivity of nations has always occurred in spite of imperialism, rather than because of it.

The Diefenbaker paradox: A man endowed with a republican heart and monarchical principles. Above: Diefenbaker and President Eisenhauer signing the Columbia River Treaty in 1961.

Below: Diefenbaker and his idol Queen Elizabeth II at Windsor Castle in 1960

John G. Diefenbaker Centre, Saskatoon, Canada, image number JGD1300

For the British Empire, an undesirable consequence of its own propaganda is that, on occasion, certain dupes tend to believe it to the point that they actually desire progress and freedom without themselves wanting to be imperialist. When the conditions and opportunities for national improvements and the promotion of the General Welfare present themselves, such personalities tend to jump boldly for them. Understanding this personality type would be necessary to understand John Diefenbaker, and his failure as a leader in a time of revolutionary change.

## Hints of a Vision

Diefenbaker's Conservatives would unseat the Liberals in 1957, coming to power as a minority government. Piercing through the anti-American rhetoric, a sense of substance, of new frontiers and national development could be detected throughout Diefenbaker's campaign. This was something completely absent from the rhetoric of all those "new nationalists" arising out of the CIIA networks.

Though promises of growth, northern expansion, and social justice were themes throughout these elections, it was not yet clear for anyone how such ideals would be attained, nor even if true intentions lay behind the fiery words which spurned the heart of the electorate to hope. Were such words to take the form of action, then it was understood by Diefenbaker and his collaborators that a new election would need be called immediately in order to win a strong majority [6].

Diefenbaker's program for Canada would be crafted with the aid of a tight group of collaborators known as his "brain trust". Among the most influential of this brain trust was a young economist named Meryl Menzies who would construct a bold agriculture policy, and former head of the Saskatchewan Progressive Conservatives Alvin Hamilton, who would lead the strategy for Northern development alongside Menzies. Other important figures would include George Hees, Donald Fleming, Roy Faibish and Gordon Churchill, all of whom maintained close correspondence with the best minds of industry and science in advancing what would soon come to be known as "the New National Policy".

# The National Policy

On February 12, 1958, the new election campaign was kicked off with a speech which set a firm theme that would spark the frontier spirit of Canadians from coast to coast, and laid out a bold plan crafted by his brain trust. Speaking to a rally of 5,000 supporters in Winnipeg words, a vision unheard and unseen in Canadian history swept across the imaginations of all those attending:

*"We intend to launch for the future, we have laid the foundations now, the long range objectives of this party. We ask from you a mandate; a new and a stronger mandate, to pursue the planning and to carry to fruition our new national development program for Canada. .. This national development policy will create a new sense of national purpose and national destiny.*

*"One Canada. One Canada, wherein Canadians will have preserved to them the control of their own economic and political destiny. Sir John A. Macdonald gave his life to this party. He opened the West. He saw Canada from East to West. I see a new Canada- a Canada of the North. What are these new principles? What are our objectives? What do we propose? We propose to assist the provinces, with their cooperation, in the financing and construction of job-creating projects necessary for the new development, where such projects are beyond the resources of the*

*provinces. We will assist the provinces with their cooperation in the conservation of the renewable natural resources. We will aid in projects which are self-liquidating. We will aid in projects which, while not self-liquidating will lead to the development of the national resources for the opening of Canada's northland. We will open that northland for development by improving transportation and communication and by the development of power, by the building of access roads. We will make an inventory of our hydroelectric potential."*

*"Ladies and gentlemen, we now intend to bring in legislation to encourage progressively increasing processing of our domestic raw materials in Canada, rather than shipping them out in raw material form. We will ensure that Canada's national resources are used to benefit Canadians and that Canadians have an opportunity to participate in Canada's development. We have not discouraged foreign investment, but we will encourage the partnership of the foreign investors with the Canadian people... This is the message I give you my fellow Canadians, not one of defeatism. Jobs! Jobs for hundreds of thousands of Canadian people. A new vision! A new hope! A new soul for Canada,"*

With this new vision for a transformed Canada, Diefenbaker stormed the campaign trail and beat all expectations by winning every single province in Canada but one. Never before had the Canadian population heard such boldness from a Prime Minister. For most of its history, Canada had been a nation founded upon moderate complacency, while bold risk taking and visionary leaders were for the Americans. Canadians were supposed to be shaped by a British constitution, and not of a revolutionary stock. The British Empire's satisfaction of having disposed of the troublesome influence C.D. Howe was suddenly made more complicated.

The greatest surprise of all was to be seen in Maurice Duplessis' Quebec, which had been a Liberal stronghold on the Federal scene since the days of Confederation and Wilfrid Laurier. With the cunning organizing by Daniel Johnson Sr., then minister of Natural Resources under Duplessis' Union

National government, Diefenbaker's Conservatives were able to win the 1958 elections with 60% of the Quebec vote. Daniel Johnson would become a strong ally of Diefenbaker during a Conference of Commonwealth Parliamentarians in 1950 and would be known as *"Diefenbaker's right hand in Quebec"* [7].

With Daniel Johnson and Maurice Duplessis' support on the east coast, and British Columbia Premier W.A.C Bennett's support in the west, Diefenbaker's Conservatives were able to sweep the March 1958 elections winning 208 out of 265 federal seats. This would be the largest majority government in Canadian history. Throughout Johnson and Bennett's leadership, both Quebec and British Columbia would lead the world in hydroelectric power development and industrialization.

# The Policy Defined

Basing their conception on their limited understanding of the first National Policy of John A. Macdonald in 1878, Diefenbaker's Brain Trust would first outline the "One Canada" program in a 1957 pamphlet entitled *"A New National Policy"* which elaborated the Party platform and five key components of the Northern Vision;

### 1- National Resource Policy

a) *Every encouragement must be given to the processing of domestic raw materials in Canada to a much greater degree than exists today;*

b) *Foreign investment must not be discouraged, but it must be directed to the maximum benefit of Canada*

c) *Canadian subsidiaries of foreign concerns... should be required to provide a substantial interest in their equity stock to Canadian investors*

d)... *wherever possible foreign companies should employ Canadian in senior management and technical posts.*

## 2- National Energy Board

*To meet the industrial demands of Canada's future I believe that there is need now for the setting up of a Canadian Energy Board... to the end that the most effective use of the energy resources of Canada in the interests of the public welfare may be assured.*

## 3- Roads to Resources

*A National Highway policy should be launched to provide highways for peace and development wherein the Federal Government will make contributions to or share in cooperation with the provinces. The challenge of Communism now and in the years ahead demands that our vast northern resources be made accessible and available to industry, for vast resources undeveloped and hidden in the earth will not fashion or forge the shield of freedom or contribute to the survival of the Free World.*

## 4-Tax Structure to be Revised

*I believe that the entire tax structure in Canada needs to be overhauled with a view to providing encouragement to the promotion of primary and secondary industries in our country.*

## 5-A Fair Share for Farmers

*We will assure the farmer of his fair share of the national income by maintaining a flexible price support program to ensure an adequate parity for agricultural producers based on a fair price-cost relationship... Agriculture and its welfare is a basic cornerstone of our policy"* [8].

On top of this program, by 1958 Diefenbaker would announce $75 million for the construction of an advanced industrial-science research city of Frobisher Bay deep within the Northwest Territories that would accommodate 4,500 citizens and their families with all of the comfort of Toronto. His monetary policy would involve tax cuts for small businesses, increasing federal grants for hospital construction from $1,000 to $2,000 per bed, increased payments to provinces by $87 million/year. $286 million would be required to assist Atlantic Provinces in energy development. A major public work would become the century old plan to construct the South Saskatchewan Dam requiring government support totaling $182 million. This project would irrigate 500 thousand acres in the Prairies, and supply 475 million kw/year to power the new Rural Electrification Program and Midwest industrial growth. Sweeping price controls, advanced payments to farmers and parity pricing were also instituted to protect the farmers from foreign dumping as well as stimulate increased production. In all, public works expenditures alone would total $1,185 million according to this first budget.

Diefenbaker's outlook to Arctic development was not limited to mineral extraction, but also included scientific research. Six components of his science program would involve [9]:

1)  Polar Continental Shelf explorations which would begin in 1959

2)  A 10 year program of magnetic survey of the Cordillera and Canadian Shield

3)  Completion of the gravity meter shield of the same area

4)  The doubling of the hydrographic survey capability

5)  The establishment of an Oceanography institute

The Fight for a Canadian Credit System

With a broad vision for the future growth of the nation thus outlined, the problem of financing immediately posed itself. This problem was compounded by several factors at once:

**1)  The deep recession which had begun in the beginning of 1958 had set in, wrecking havoc on employment, and making private capital scarce for such long term endeavours.**

**2)  The resistance of James Coyne, Governor of the Bank of Canada to any such investment programs**

**3)  The maturation of the first waves of World War II "Victory Bonds" which demanded $10 billion from 1958-68. to pay for World War II.**

Before the first budget could be presented by Finance Minister Donald Fleming, the problem of the Victory Bonds had to be resolved. Net expenses would require $1.423 billion, with $1.950 billion required to pay for the first wave of maturing securities for a total of $3.4 billion total that year. From January 1, 1959 to September 1, 1966, $10 billion in Victory Bonds would mature at 3% interest. $400 billion would need to be borrowed from the Bank of Canada for debt payment alone. The problem was absolutely untenable.

The solution to this problem could not be found within the confines of any monetarist thinking dominant in Canada at that time. A creative change was required, and a concept outside of the space defined by the problem was demanded. This would be a feat that Diefenbaker and his brain trust would accomplish with the Conversion Loan of 1958. This solution would demand Federal loans to finance the conversion of those maturing bonds to the tune of $6.4 billion and transform the debt incurred to win World War II, into productive debt that would be "self-liquidating" in the financing of Canada's development! During a radio announcement of July 14, 1958, Diefenbaker would outline his view of the role of credit within a developing system;

*"This, the largest financial project in our history, offers an opportunity to all holders of victory bonds which were purchased as an act of patriotic faith during the war years, to re-invest them for the greater development of greater Canada. These monies that were advanced during the days of war, and which contributed to the victory, we now ask to be made available to speed the pace of peaceful progress and the program of national development... The action we are taking will make it possible for our nation to embark on a new era of peacetime prosperity far and beyond anything we have ever known. I sincerely believe that great objectives can and will be attained by the faith and enterprise of all our people. To that end, your Government believes that the steps we are taking are necessary in order to create the climate in which this can come to full fruition...*

*In saying that a major result of this new load is to make other necessary funds*

**Fig. 1:1958 Frobisher Bay Domed City design (commissioned by the Dept. of Public Works)**

Centre de recherche Lionel-Groulx, P46/T1,10.13.

Diefenbaker's bold vision for a new national policy driven by northern development exemplified by the nuclear powered domed city of Frobisher Bay (above), financed by the Bank of Canada (image below) won him the support of such leading nation builders as Quebec's Premiers Maurice Duplessis and Daniel Johson (featured above right and middle), as well as British Columbia's great Premier W.A.C. Bennett (bottom right)

Faculté de droit – Université de Montréal

Canadian Museum of History

*available for immediate participation by the federal government in the development of resources, I need hardly remind you that such participation is not, by any means, an end in itself. Its chief objective is, of course, to provide essentials such as access roads, railroads, and energy sources and the business climate which will attract private investment to newly developing and lesser developed regions in our country, in amounts many times in excess of the government investment. It is confidently expected that the debt refinancing which we announced today will clear the decks for greatly increased private investment in our future, just as surely as it will do so for government investment."[10]*

This would be the first self-conscious idea in Canadian history where a National Bank would be used for the purpose of generating anti-inflationary credit driven by a greater national mission in a time of peace. Up until this point, this principle had been first successfully expressed under the 1st and 2nd National Banking system of Alexander Hamilton and Nicholas Biddle, Abraham Lincoln's Hamiltonian credit system of "greenbacks" during the Civil War, and Franklin Roosevelt's use of the Reconstruction Finance Corporation during the New Deal. Nothing could induce such fear in the British Empire than witnessing its own prize colony in North America adopt an outlook and mechanism for carrying it out whose nature was to bring it to a truly sovereign status alongside Britain's mortal enemy.

Sadly, the full fruition of this policy would not be permitted to come into being.

## The Coyne Affair

Diefenbaker and his finance minister would require full cooperation from the Bank of Canada in order for the New National Policy to succeed.

Since the Bank of Canada (unlike the Federal Reserve in the United States) was made a 100% publicly owned entity after its nationalization in 1937, it was reasonable for either man to believe that it would be a cooperative instrument in the national mission. What they didn't realize however, was the role that such British agents were playing within the top echelons of Canada's Civil Service in undermining nation building strategies. In the case of the Bank of Canada's Governor James Coyne, Diefenbaker found an enemy that would publicly battle his policy to the point of creating a national scandal resulting in Coyne's dismissal in 1961.

Coyne, an Oxford trained Rhodes Scholar was an early disciple to the synthetic New Nationalism expounded by the likes of Vincent Massey and Walter Gordon. As a nationalist, he believed and preached publicly for policies that would choke American industry from access to the Canadian markets during a speech in 1958, Coyne expounded his views:

*"We are now, at one of the more critical crossroads in our history, perhaps the most critical of all, when economic developments and preoccupation with economic doctrines of an earlier age are pushing us down the road that leads to loss of any effective power to be masters in our own household and ultimate absorption in and by another..."*[11]

While vigorously touring Canada, calling for lines of foreign investment to be cut off in the defense of Canadian sovereignty, and demanding the nation learn to live off of its own resources, Coyne never proposed how his propositions would be accomplished. In fact, being a devout monetarist, Coyne worshipped the "balanced budget". Extolling a policy of "tight money", Coyne believed that the recession could only be ended if Canada would only cut the budget, and pay its debts. Commenting on Coyne's ideology, Diefenbaker remarked in his Memoirs:

*"Our economic projections indicated that unemployment would remain a serious problem until at least 1961. Coyne was content to assume that the level of*

*demand would be adequate for sustained growth if our economic policy embraced the goal of "sound money". He apparently belonged to the economic school which had considered that the only way out of the great depressions was to have more depression and the only way to cure unemployment was to have more unemployment."*

By the time Coyne was in control of the Bank of Canada, the "Harris Doctrine" had already been created by the previous Minister of Finance which held that there were two sovereignties in Canadian economics: the Government and the Bank of Canada. This policy of dual jurisdiction of sovereignty would give Coyne the confidence to resist the government, and criticize its fiscal policy until the expected demand for his resignation struck.

The Coyne affair would eventually result in a train wreck for Diefenbaker. Of all of the absurd policies Coyne represented which ran against the intention of his administration, Diefenbaker chose to use Coyne's acceptance of a pension increase from 13 to 25 thousand dollars. While the pension increase was certainly slimy, it followed legal protocol, giving Coyne the moral upper hand in the public inquiries that would ensue. Who it was that advised Diefenbaker to fire Coyne on this populist basis is still not known, but the effect of this choice would haunt Diefenbaker during the coming months, as Coyne would be elevated by the mass media to the status of a folk hero fighting as a David against Goliath[12].

Instead of stepping down as per the request of both the Cabinet and the Bank's Board of Directors, Coyne held a press conference revealing that he was being unlawfully prosecuted by Diefenbaker in order to take the blame for any failure in economic policy up until this point. A protracted fight between Coyne and the government ensued with a bill even passing in parliament forcing his replacement. Fleming would comment on the situation: *"Coyne had declared war on the government... his actions were part of a clearly calculated attempt to build up controversy"* [13].

The Liberal opposition under Lester B. Pearson and the mass media colluded with Coyne to shape popular opinion against Diefenbaker. By the time Coyne officially stepped down in July 1961, a reported 60% of the 76% of the population that had heard of the affair sided with Coyne, and only 9% sided with Diefenbaker[14]. Coyne was even named "newsmaker of the year for 1961" by the Canadian Press. It is undoubtedly the case that the drop from 208 to 116 federal seats in the 1962 elections would be the effect of this scandal. With the majority now lost, Diefenbaker's minority government was susceptible to a vote of no-confidence triggering a snap election at any moment.

The multiple crises and absurd public relations disasters arising out of the breakdown of U.S.-Canadian relations following the Coyne affair compounded the crisis in the public's faith in its government to the point that the elections of 1963 resulted in Diefenbaker's fall from power. This process contributed to the failure of the full intention of the "conversion loan/credit system" plan of 1958. Much of the Northern Vision's steam was lost during the period following the Coyne debacle as more and more energy was consumed in putting out diplomatic and economic fires set by the general dynamic of the Cold War.

# Diefenbaker's Fallout with Kennedy

It is perhaps one of the greatest misfortunes that two men so dedicated to the cause of human progress would find themselves so deeply at odds with each other as Diefenbaker and John Kennedy. Indeed Robert F. Kennedy would say that *"my brother really hated only two men in all his presidency. One was Sukarno [president of Indonesia] and the other was Diefenbaker".*

The factors contributing to this schism are manifold, and it will be the purpose of another report to investigate more in depth all of those variables both economic, military and philosophical that fed the break between the two leaders during this important period of world history. For the time being it is worth mentioning, if only summarily, several of the key points of US–Canada conflict:

1) Diefenbaker's reneging on his earlier commitment (with Eisenhower) to host nuclear warheads upon the American made Bomarc missiles that had replaced the Avro Arrow missile delivery system (see appendix).

2) Canada's refusal to participate in trade embargos with communist China and Cuba as per the demands of Kennedy [15].

3) Kennedy's refusal to tell Canada about its decision to enact a blockade on Soviet entry to Cuban waters, and Diefenbaker's refusal to acknowledge the nuclear threat posed during the Cuban missile crisis of 1962. This would be followed by his rejection of the US demand that Canada activate its NORAD forces for potential war with the Soviets. Minister of Defence Douglass Harkness would ignore the Prime Minister and move the Canadian military into position anyway.

4) Diefenbaker's refusal to join the Organization of American States (OAS), and Kennedy's 1961 speech in Ottawa calling for Canada to join even after being refused by the Prime Minister.

Subjectively, both Diefenbaker and Kennedy derived their sense of mission and commitment to progress from opposing historical perspectives. Where Kennedy's identity was firmly grounded in the superiority of the American system of republicanism, Diefenbaker derived his identity from the belief in the superiority of the British system.

Objectively, the global tension caused by the Cold War's policy of Mutually Assured Destruction defined the behaviour and necessarily neurotic mindset of many leading military figures, and statesmen during this period. The fact that civilization could be annihilated at any given moment would weigh heavily upon every decision made during this time, making disagreements and mistrust between nations that much more existential in nature. Such problems between the USA and Canada during this period were not lacking, and historians agree that never have relations sunk to such lows as they had during the interval of 1960-62.

Certainly, if these men had a better sense of the factors driving the environment in which they were operating during this time, the powerful collaboration of Canada and the USA based on a continental perspective of nation building, vectored around vast water and energy projects pursued by JFK such as the North American Water and Power Alliance would have shaped the course of history in a very different way. But that was not to be.

## Iago's Ghost Haunts North America

The fact that top advisors trusted by both men during this time were simultaneously British Agents is also an important fact to bear in mind. While Kennedy had suffered such scoundrels as National Security advisor McGeorge Bundy, campaign advisor George Ball, CIA director John Foster Dulles whispering in his ear, and attempting to shape his perception of reality, Diefenbaker was also not lacking in his share of Iagos. From the Rhodes Scholar and Justice Minister Davie Fulton, and his group of "technocrats" who would go on to reform the Liberal Party under Trudeau to Diefenbaker's trusted Clerk of the Privy Council R.B. Bryce, Diefenbaker would lament years later of the problem:

*"I have often been asked why I appointed those people to Cabinet who had so vigorously opposed my leadership. Abraham Lincoln, who had included several in his cabinet who had been strong and bitter antagonists, was asked why he had done so. He is reported to have replied to the effect that he liked to have them around so he could see what they were doing. Unfortunately I trusted my colleagues."[16]*

Due to the sage guidance of the likes of Dwight Eisenhower, Eleanor Roosevelt, Gen. Douglas MacArthur and President De Gaulle, JFK soon lost his naïve faith in many agents working within his Cabinet evidenced by his firing of CIA director John Foster Dulles in 1962. Although not having the benefit of many of such positive influences, in later years, Diefenbaker would illustrate his awareness of subversive agents infesting the upper levels of the Civil Service who had worked to undermine his administration from within:

*"The Civil Service is there to advise on, but not to determine policy. A minister is there to see that government policy is carried out within his department... That said, had I been returned to office in 1965, there would have been some major changes made. It became obvious as soon as we were out of office in 1963 that there were quite a number of senior people in the public service, about whom I had not known, who had simply been underground, quietly working against my government and waiting for the Liberals to return to power"[17]*

# The Success and the Tragedy

While the Diefenbaker government would fall in February 1963 after a vote of "no confidence" by the Liberals under Lester B Pearson, and many of the institutions that were created under the Conservatives were soon undone, it cannot be said that Diefenbaker's New National Policy was a complete disaster.

The development of the South Saskatchewan Dam dramatically increased the agro-industrial productivity of the Prairies while the Agriculture Rehabilitation and Development Act revolutionized Canadian agriculture. And while the design of the modern northern city of Frobisher Bay would never become reality, over 4,000 miles of roads were created in the Northern provinces and territories under the "Roads to Resources" program. The Pine Point Railway was also completed along with the advancement of the Trans-Canada Highway.

From the standpoint of social justice, under Diefenbaker, aboriginals were finally given the right to the vote. The Canadian Bill of Rights of 1960 became the first and only constitutional document in Canadian history founded on principle before legality or utilitarianism and advanced the protection of the individual far beyond anything that had come before. The fact that Diefenbaker would attempt to reconcile this new principled law of the land with the absolute power vested in the provinces set out in section 92 of the imperial BNA Act of 1867, left the Bill of Rights without the means of becoming a reality.

While many factors can be attributed to the failure and sabotage of the New National Policy and Northern Vision, none is more important than the complete lack of understanding Diefenbaker suffered regarding the true essence of empire which defined the context in which he operated. His passion would often govern his reason and thus both would perpetually be corrupted by this mistaken belief that there could be a reasonable justification for "the divine right of kings" and the British system's superiority over that of the American system.

Diefenbaker's populism would also serve to sabotage his own agenda in ways he never could have imagined. In leaping into power on a wave of anti–Americanism, he could not refute the Coynes, Gordons, Fultons or other "New Nationalists" both in government and the press who accused him of not presenting to the public those means by which a full development strategy for his vision could become possible. Both Diefenbaker and his opponents alike understood that without broad American investment, and without the successful conversion of WW II Victory Bonds into new development bonds, then his plans could not come to fruition.

Believing the parliamentary system to be superior to the republican system, Diefenbaker mistakenly gave undo flexibility to members of his own party to vote as they saw fit, and attempted to bring every policy measure to a vote in parliament before becoming law. This behaviour would be in stark contrast to the C.D. Howe method of statecraft under the 1935-1957 Liberals. C.D. Howe had long made his disdain for parliamentary democracy known to all and used the "presidential" authority of the war measures act as the primary driver of Canadian development, bypassing the circus of parliamentary partisanship and unprincipled bickering as much as possible while keeping the Civil Service and members of his party on as tight a leash as possible. Diefenbaker's commitment to parliamentary "democracy" would give his enemies both within and without of government every opportunity to sabotage his policies at every turn.

For all of his failings, the pure substance of the Diefenbaker vision was well illustrated in his final appearance during the 1963 election campaign:

*"I just want to leave one thing with you. You have had a government in Canada this past six years that has a simple philosophy, an old philosophy. That's to build Canada. Not by worshipping statistics, but by watching for areas and people that need help- that's the One Canada, One Nation basis. Our task for the net two or three hundred years is going to be moving from the south into the north, so that future generations will know that we have not forgotten the principles upon which*

*this nation was founded and which generation after generation have had to stand together to protect"*

# The London-steered "Deep State" that ran the coup

Oxford-trained Rhodes Scholars Davie Fulton (top left), and James Coyne- the deposed Governor of the Bank of Canada whom Diefenbaker fired in 1960 (top right) Governor General Vincent Massey (bottom left) did much to oversee the coup while Masey's former assistant Walter Gordon (bottom right) cleansed the liberal party of all "pro-growth" C.D. Howe liberals. All of these figures were leading representatives of the "new nationalism" movement which arose in 1963

# Epilogue:
# The Palace Revolution in the Liberal Party

When the Diefenbaker administration fell in 1963, the Liberal Party that returned to power under Lester B. Pearson was a far cry from that which had fallen in 1957. During the interim of Diefenbaker's government, the Liberal Party was to be re-organized directly by Walter Lockhart Gordon, the British Foreign Office's agent working through the CIIA.

During this period, Gordon would prove to become the most powerful man in the Liberal Party and the controller of Prime Minister Lester B. Pearson. Gordon would lead the cleansing of all C.D. Howe Liberals and transform the Party from the pro-American machine it had been since WW II into a radically anti-American, anti-progress colony under British financial control. The recommendations that Gordon had made in his 1957 Royal Commission Report on Economic Prospects for Canada, especially those regarding restricting American investments and ownership of Canadian industry, would now, for the most part, be fully supported.

In his memoirs, John Diefenbaker noted the irony of Walter Gordon's radical promotion of Canadian nationalism on the one side, yet hatred of the policies pushed by Diefenbaker which would provide the actual means of attaining those nationalist ends which Gordon apparently desired:

*"One of the ironies of recent Canadian history is that Walter Gordon, a man whom I only met for a few minutes when he delivered to me his Royal Commission Report, has stated that he decided to do everything in his power to make Mr. Pearson Prime Minister because he hated me and feared that my policies would wreck Canada!" (FN: p. 202, Diefenbaker Memoirs)*

Gordon went much further in his attacks on Diefenbaker when, after declaring his commitment to overthrow the Conservative government, he said that the Tory leader *"does remind me of Hitler who was far more dangerous"* (FN: p.71 Gordon Rise of New Nationalism).

Lester B. Pearson, also a Rhodes Scholar and former assistant in London to Vincent Massey in the Canadian High Commission during WW II, would become the vehicle Gordon would select to oversee the transformation of the Liberal Party and the purging of pro-development Liberals who would resist the isolationist monetary policies of Gordon. One of those who would suffer the purge was Henry Erskine Kidd, General Secretary for the Liberal Party who would refer to the process led by Gordon as *"a palace revolution"*[18].

Under Pearson, Gordon would become Finance Minister from 1963 to 1965 and then President of the Privy Council from 1967 to 1968. Although Gordon's attempts at reforming the Canadian economy during that time frame would fail, creating an eventual rift between himself and Pearson, the damage was done to the Liberal Party and the Canadian national spirit alike. The population became jaded to bold visions of progress, and the political structures became crusted with layers of bureaucratic machinery that would increasingly hide the anti-human ideologies of population control and world governance from both the population and even the policy-makers who would apply many of those destructive programs which would only begin to take full force by the following decade. The wound was made large enough and the white blood cells weakened to the point that the infection could take over without much effective resistance.

This transition would also bring various neo-Malthusian ideologues and technocrats into powerful positions of the Liberal Party, first within the province of Quebec during the "Quiet Revolution" and then on the federal level, with the rise of Walter Gordon's "New Nationalism". This transition would sow the seeds for the next stage in the imperial paradigm shift with the 1968 "Cybernetics Revolution" of Fabian Society asset Pierre Elliot Trudeau and his colleagues Gérard Pelletier, Jean Marchand and René Lévesque

# CHAPTER III – WHO WAS WALTER LOCKHART GORDON?

Walter Lockhart Gordon's legacy typifies the Delphic methods applied by the British Empire to subvert the cultures of their victim populations. Walter Gordon's master's understood that in order to maintain a modern empire, both the greatest control of a victim population must occur while maintaining the greatest illusion of democracy. This is only possible to the degree that the perception of a victim is as far removed from their sad reality as possible. Gordon's role in shaping the current of Canadian history is so strong, that a brief biography is in order before proceeding to the substance of this report.

While Gordon was an executive director of the Canadian Institute for International Affairs (CIIA- formerly the Rhodes-Milner Roundtable Group), he was known to be one of Canada's wealthiest entrepreneurs, having inherited the reins to Clarkson Gordon from his father in the 1940s. For a time, Clarkson Gordon was the largest management consulting and accounting firm in Canada. Gordon became involved in the Canadian government during World War II when he worked alongside a young Lester B. Pearson on the Price Spreads Royal Commission of 1942. After becoming close friends, Pearson was assigned to work under the control of CIIA chief Vincent Massey in the London High Commission for the duration of WW II. In 1955, Gordon was assigned by his London masters to head the Royal Commission on Canada's Economic Prospects. This Royal Commission produced the first report of its kind by officially painting America as an Empire poised to take over the Canadian economy. The report called for a new economic strategy to cut America off from the Canadian economy even if it meant a lowering of living standards for Canadians! This report was joined by a sister Royal Commission conducted earlier under the leadership of CIIA leader Vincent Massey calling for the need to create a synthetic Canadian culture for fear of the "Americanization" of the Canadian identity. Both reports were promoted by the Canadian press and rapidly polarized the Canadian population into largely becoming paranoid of America's immanent takeover [1]. The rampant anti-Americanism became the foundation for the policies that followed in the subsequent decades.

After helping to organize the downfall of the well-intentioned, but highly misguided Conservative government of John Diefenbaker, which fell in 1963, Gordon organized a complete cleansing of all pro-development "C.D. Howe Liberals" and brought in a new breed of technocrats to begin a revolution in bureaucratic affairs under the guidance of the newly formed Organization of Economic Cooperation and Development (OECD) headed by Club of Rome co-founder Alexander King. During this time, Gordon was fully in control of Lester B. Pearson, having taken Pearson's leash from Vincent Massey in the 1950s. Gordon had organized Pearson to head the Liberal Party ever since 1949, writing to Pearson in 1955 that *"I have a feeling that people would like to follow your star in droves- if and when you decide the time is right to give them the nod."* [2]. Before even becoming a member of the Liberal Party, Gordon even paid for a large scale Nobel Prize gala in Pearson's honour from his own pocket in 1958 [3].

By this time, Gordon was officially the kingmaker and controller of Pearson under whom he served as Minister of Finance from 1963-1965. Revisionist historian and Gordon protégé Peter Newman described his role during this time as being "in undisputed command of the liberal policy apparatus. Nearly every initiative taken during the 60 days was inspired by the Minister of Finance". It was in this powerful position during the first "60 days" that Gordon began to apply the "nationalist" financial measures prescribed in his 1957 Royal Commission Report to limit foreign investment limits and cut off "continentalist" forces that were seeking greater US-Canadian involvement around a nation building paradigm.

The greatest threat from the continentalist forces centered around the continental approach to water and energy resource management provoked by the efforts of President Dwight D. Eisenhower, whose allies in Canada included B.C Premier W.A.C. Bennett and C.D. Howe. Eisenhower's water management plans were announced for the first time in his 1955 address, and again re-iterated in his 1960 State of the Union. The political climate created by the strong intention to deal with water scarcity decades before the crisis was to strike inspired the design of the North American Water and Power Alliance (NAWAPA) by the Parson's Corporation in 1955. This orientation to breaking out of those closed parameters of water scarcity was advanced boldly by the likes of John F. Kennedy, and his brother Robert. RFK even endorsed the NAWAPA resolution introduced by Senator Frank Moss.

After two years, his economic program turned out to be such a disaster that Gordon was forced to resign from his position, only to become President of the Privy Council Office (1966-68) where he set the stage for the second purge of the Liberal Party and re-organization of the Privy Council Office which occurred in 1968.

It was this second purge which saw Fabian socialist asset Pierre Elliot Trudeau, Jean Marchand and Gerald Pelletier brought in to prominent positions within the federal Liberal Party. Even though Gordon preferred Marchand (Pearson's lieutenant in Quebec) to Trudeau, he became an early backer of Trudeau nonetheless. By 1967, Lester Pearson was considered compromised as he was too easily influenced by the anti-Gordon faction in the Liberal Party, and resigned due to "health reasons".

Pearson's incapacity to speak French had also contributed to making him incapable of dealing with the republican nationalist ferment created in

Quebec under Premier Daniel Johnson Sr., and exacerbated by French President Charles de Gaulle's intervention into Quebec in July 1967. De Gaulle sent shockwaves through Canada and the world when he called for a "Quebec libre" as a pillar to a global 'Francophonie' founded upon scientific and technological progress. After successfully attacking Johnson in a public debate, followed by a successful assignment coercing French speaking African leaders to ignore de Gaulle's strategy in favour of a 'Canadian option', Pierre Trudeau was quickly rewarded by being made Prime Minister following a social engineering campaign seemingly modelled on Beatlemania.

# CHAPTER IV – THE DE GAULLE/JOHNSON INTERVENTION TO SAVE THE SOUL OF QUEBEC

*"It were wise to examine what opportunities exist to replace the British based parliamentary system with a congressional system based upon the American model".*

-Daniel Johnson Sr., Premier of Quebec

[This chapter was co-written with Quebec-based historian Raynald Rouleau]

# CH. IV PART 1 – THE ORIGINS OF THE PARTI QUÉBÉCOIS

The founders of the Parti Québecois (PQ) never had the intention of transforming Quebec into a truly sovereign country: that is to say, a constitutional republic, independent of the British Empire. A republic that would be built upon the inalienable rights of citizens, as these were defined and later enshrined in the preamble of the United States Constitution by the founding fathers of the American republic, as the right to life, liberty and the pursuit of happiness.

We are not referencing the actual leaders of the PQ, but rather those who, from the beginning, catalyzed the PQ into existence and continue, to this day, to forge and profit from the artificial divisions that were partly successful in setting up the larger segment of the population of Quebec, the French speakers against the English speaking Canadians living in Quebec and the rest of Canada. A perceived unbridgeable divide that was famously called The Two Solitudes, in earlier times.

In fact, these catalyzers of the separatist movement had fought tooth and nail against Daniel Johnson Sr. who was among the leading nation-builders in Canadian history and one who did have a mission to implement a constitutional republic for Canada modeled on the American constitution.

The PQ was created 16 days after the tragic death of Daniel Johnson, the then Premier of Quebec. The goal was simple: attract all separatist-nationalist forces; whether they be left, right, communist, socialist, catholic or Masonic. The game plan was straightforward: maintain the separatist movement as a wedge issue, a divide and conquer British Empire tactic and prevent a Johnson solution that would overthrow the British stranglehold over Canada.

In 1982, the LaRouche authored Draft Proposal for a Commonwealth of Canada was also an attempt to free all Canadians from British imperial control. Now, over 35 years later, the required policy is called the Glass-Steagall system that would eliminate speculative banking and create a Canadian National Bank, on Hamilton's model, that would issue large amounts of productive public credit that would transform Canada into a fully sovereign nation-state.

## The Queen's Crown Agents

One of the impediments to a sovereign Canada has been an aspect of the Monarchy's extension into its colonies and beyond which is of exceptional importance for Canadians and Quebecois to become familiar with: Her Majesty's Crown Agents.

Before Canada was ever given the legal status of "country", the term in usage was "Dominion of Canada"; an appendage of the British Empire within the North American continent, administered by Crown Agents, across hundreds of institutions.

This structure still exists to this day, and in certain ways, exercises an even greater influence today. *"Crown Agents have no formal Constitution and are not part of the United Kingdom Civil Service or of the United Kingdom Government machine... Crown agents act as businesses and financial agents for the Governments of all territories for the administration of which the Secretary of State is ultimately responsible, including the territories under the protection of Her Majesty and the territories administered on behalf of the United Nations"* [1].

Crown Agents work directly through such key organizations that run the upper echelons of the Civil Service, as well as the Canadian Institute for International Affairs. These bodies coordinate directly with the Canadian oligarchy and London's Foreign Office through the Canadian Council of Chief Executives. It is not within the corporate boards of directors or even parliament, but here in this hive, where the real directing power of Canada is located.

As for the Parti Québécois itself, it was founded by René Lévesque. During World War II, Lévesque was recruited by an agent going by the name of Robb, who was the Montreal bureau chief of the Office of War Information [2] (OWI), a nominally American intelligence service, but which operated under British control [3]. Lévesque was sent to New York to meet Pierre Lazareff, the editor-in-chief of the French services of the OWI. He was quickly sent to London. By the end of the war he had attained the equivalent to the level of captain: *"We were still among the best paid guys. I had something equivalent to the grade of lieutenant. I think I ended as a captain. I wasn't a captain in charge of a unit, but something equivalent"* said René Lévesque in an interview years later [4]. After this experience, he was recruited by British intelligence as a "journalist" for the Montreal office of the international radio service of the Canadian Broadcasting Corporation (CBC). He was transferred to television services in the 1950s and became a celebrity for the French Canadians with his popular political-economic news program "Point de Mire" on Radio Canada.

During the 1950s and early 1960s, Lévesque was a regular contributor to the magazine Cité Libre begun by his school period friend, Pierre Elliot Trudeau. By this time, Trudeau had also been recruited by British Intelligence after his conditioning at Harvard, and the London School of Economics. Trudeau was tutored by mentors like William Yandell Elliot, Joseph Schumpeter, Wassily Leontieff, and the leader of the British Fabian Society Harold Laski.

Both young men had been profiled early on in their Jesuit-run elitist schools; Trudeau in Collège Jean-de-Brébeuf and Levesque in la Séminaire de Gaspé . The idea that there had been a legitimate feud between these two men in later years would become one of the greatest frauds of Canadian history.

It was at this moment that Lévesque was "officially" catapulted to action in Quebec politics. The reason was very simple. It was vital to end, at all cost, the power of the Union Nationale as Daniel Johnson was in the midst of becoming its leader, after the sudden deaths of Maurice Duplessis and Paul Sauvé and the failure of Antonio Barrette as leader of the party. With Daniel Johnson as leader, the Union Nationale would again win the elections of 1966. From the British point of view, this could absolutely not be allowed to happen. Daniel Johnson was after all, a politician of Irish descent, who understood history, and most importantly understood the psychology of the British Empire, especially how the Empire had caused the Irish to suffer famine over generations as a matter of policy. Johnson was part of a small but influential group working within the Catholic Church, who opposed the massive introduction of Malthusian values into society via the Organization of Economic Cooperation and Development (OECD) which had forced school reforms leading to the brainwashing of youth in all industrialized countries. This was the beginning of what was later called "the counter culture revolution" of sex, drugs and Rock & Roll [5].

After the Liberal victory in Quebec's 1960 elections, René Lévesque, and another Brébeuf classmate Paul Guérin-Lajoie were among the new `reformers` assigned to carry out the overhaul of the Quebec political and educational structure. Oxford Rhodes Scholar Paul Guérin-Lajoie, the first Minister of Education, would lead the radical reforms of the Quebec educational system that brought in those OECD reforms by 1965.

Within this small but influential group working within the Catholic Church, this "alliance for progress and development" were to be found men representing several nations, from diverse regions of the world, such as Aldo Moro of Italy, Ben Barka of Morrocco, John F. Kennedy and his brother Robert, General de Gaulle of France, Cardinal Montini (later to become Pope Paul VI), and Martin Luther King, to name but a few. All promoted human progress. For these people, every human was created in the image of God, regardless of colour and every man, woman and child had the fundamental right to development and enjoy the full fruits of scientific and technological progress. This concept is extremely dangerous for an empire which can only maintain its hegemony through the exploitation of resources, and a physical-intellectual impoverishment of its subjects.

It is within this context that René Lévesque played his assigned role, directly against the networks of Daniel Johnson. The only positive steps taken by the Liberal Party in Quebec during their period in government (1960-1966), were made via the efforts of Charles de Gaulle, his ministers, and the leader of Opposition Daniel Johnson who had many like-minded thinkers within the Liberal Party. The intensity of their organizing even influenced at times the paradoxical and confused Premier Jean Lesage who tended to see himself as a "C.D. Howe nation-builder", yet was often controlled by forces that he never understood. Little beknownst to Lesage, these forces ironically hated both progress and especially C.D. Howe, the "minister of everything" of the federal Liberal Party of 1938-1957. Lesage would have the wits about him to first open up "Maisons du Québec" in Paris with the help of Charles de Gaulle, but not nearly enough to recognize in what way he was being used to undermine both Quebec and Canada as a whole.

The majority of the financing of the Liberal Party at that time, was coming from the networks run by Maurice Strong, an enemy of Charles de Gaulle, who himself was an active agent working for the networks of Prince Philip and Prince Bernhard. Liberal Party funds were channeled through subsidiary entities controlled by Power Corporation, of which Maurice Strong was a leading director. Strong became Vice President of Power Corporation in 1963, after having made a fortune during the nationalization of electricity in Quebec. Power Corporation soon got out of the business of energy and quickly became a giant consortium specializing in financial services whose reins were given to a young Paul Desmarais to run as an integral component to the newly re-organized Canadian oligarchy in 1968.

To get a simple idea of the relationship between René Lévesque and Daniel Johnson: One day, during a session of the National Assembly, Levesque told Johnson «vous êtes le personnage le plus vomissant que je connaisse» ("you are the most disgusting person that I know").

Nevertheless, after Louis Joseph Papineau, Daniel Johnson is the political figure who did the most to advance the development of Quebec and its citizens. Johnson understood that in order for the idea of a new constitution to be accepted in Canada, it needed the approval of the other provinces, though not necessarily Ottawa. In effect, due to a fallacy imbedded in the British North America Act of 1867, the progress of Canada has tended to be catalyzed by the provinces rather than the federal government. From a legal standpoint, Ottawa was rarely much more than the "buffer" between the British Empire and the Canadians. When Ottawa had been able to direct true development as was seen clearly during the 1937–1957 Liberal Party leadership, it was due to a mix of American private and public initiative, and the vast war powers used by the likes of C.D. Howe which permitted him to bypass both the parliamentary red tape and the civil service bureaucracy long after World War II had come to an end. Daniel Johnson knew that if he could gain the support of the provinces, then Ottawa would have no other choice but to accept the will of the people.

An informal conference comprising the ten provinces had occurred by the end of 1967, in order to put in place a strategy which would go on to become the first official Constitutional conference in February 1968, which strove to adopt a Canadian Constitution, written by and for Canadians. A constitutional committee made up of provincial representatives was established in the course of that month. This committee's mandate involved studying all of the propositions made by the provinces. Sadly, on June 5, 1968, Johnson would suffer a severe heart attack, forcing him to pull out of politics for 10 weeks, returning triumphantly in September. He would give a press conference on September 25 in Quebec, just before leaving for the inauguration of the Manicouagan 5 dam, where he was planning to unveil his full nation-building vision. He was planning to meet de Gaulle ten days later, and was intending to invite him to return to Quebec in 1969. However, the next morning he would be found dead in his bed at the foot of the great hydro project that he had set into motion ten years earlier.

To add insult to injury, Charles de Gaulle would be denied an invitation to attend the funeral of "mon ami Johnson". This would mark the end of Johnson's Constitutional project.

# CH. IV PART 2 - THE CHARLES DE GAULLE / JOHNSON PROJECT

During the summer of 1967, Canada was celebrating its centennial with the 100th anniversary of the British North America Act. It must be noted that the Canadian Confederation of 1867 was formed for no other reason but the protection of the empire against the republican forces of Abraham Lincoln in the United States and their allies in Canada. That same year, the president of France would take the hand extended to him by Daniel Johnson, which would send a shockwave throughout the entire North American continent. De Gaulle received an official invitation from the Premier of Quebec in May 1967, after Mr. Johnson himself was the General's guest of honour in Paris.

During this historic meeting, France and Quebec had put an emphasis upon nine principled points of cooperation for the development of culture, technology, and industry. One of these points would involve Quebec's entry into the Franco-German space program "Symphony", for the development of communications satellites [6]. We must remember that thanks to de Gaulle, France had become a world power centering on the pillars of *"Progress, Independence and Peace"*. De Gaulle would tell the people of Quebec: "Your history is our history. In reality this is the history of France", he would add that within the circumstances *"it is now up to you to play the role which was written for you, a French role"*. This would not mean that those who spoke English or were foreign to France couldn't play a "French role". Are you inspired by the idea of "Progress, Independence and Peace"? If so, then in the mind of de Gaulle, you are French!

Continuing his voyage in Canada, de Gaulle would speak in the Town of Berthier on July 24, 1967: *"France for her part, after great obstacles and tests, is in the midst of a booming renewal and, you can see and feel it. It is an example both of progress for the world, but also an example of the service of men, wherever or whomever they are!"* Are these the words of an egotist, an ignoramus, a racist or a chauvinist as popular historians of the Empire would like you to believe?

Midway between Québec and Montreal, at the industrial city of Trois-Rivières, the General had launched a brilliant attack against the British Empire: *"When a nation is born, we cannot justify her existence and her rights, as you sung "Oh Canada" earlier, we cannot justify her existence and her rights unless we are moving towards progress. This is who you are, and I can see it from one end of Quebec to the other. You are in the midst of accomplishing magnificent economic and technological developments!"*

If we look at the world today, those countries most under-developed are those territories which are under the influence of the British Empire. The "love of progress", as de Gaulle describes it, is non-existent within the British Empire. Enslavement and the pillaging of resources are the only conditions within which the cancerous Empire can survive. But as Johnson and de Gaulle understood the problem clearly, cancerous cells have no lasting future. They die with the host which they had just killed. The greater their power, the faster their fall. A country cannot survive for long unless it is perpetually creating true wealth, unless it is progressing.

De Gaulle saw his intervention in Canada from 1960 to 1969 as not only an intervention into international geopolitics, but of primary importance for all humankind. Continuing his voyage along the shores of the St

Lawrence River, he declared during a stop in Louiseville: *"this effort (the cooperation between France and New France for progress, independence and peace), this effort is something which France wishes to develop and you can count on her, since that which we do together, we French from one side of the Atlantic to the other, is what we can do to improve humanity as a whole"*.

## "Vive le Québec Libre!"

On July 24, de Gaulle's open top presidential motorcade made several stops in small towns and villages on his journey between Quebec and Montreal on what is known as the former "Chemin du Roy" (the King's Path) along the northern shore of St Lawrence. Throughout the day, he gave several short speeches, in different town and villages, to cheering crowds. Before he reached Montreal in the early evening, he already had been enthusiastically greeted by nearly half a million people. In the evening, he delivered his famous speech from the balcony of Montreal City Hall, in front of a large crowd assembled at Place Jacques Cartier.

*"... I will confide in you a secret you should not repeat. Both this evening, and all along my journey, I have found myself in the same sort of atmosphere as I experienced during the Liberation. On top of this, I have seen what efforts have been achieved towards progress, development and consequently freedom that you have accomplished here... This is why she (France) has, alongside the government of Quebec, and alongside my friend Johnson, signed treaties to unite the French from both sides of the Atlantic... You are in the midst of becoming elites, you are creating factories, enterprises, laboratories which will surprise everyone... Long live Montreal! Long live Quebec! Long live a free Quebec! Long live a French Canada and long live France »!*

The British monarchy was frightened by the visit of de Gaulle. The awakening of the "little people", the awakening of a country, of a republic, the idea of freedom, and the integration of "that spark of France", which is diametrically opposed to the Empire, represented a mortal threat to its existence. This is why a propaganda campaign would be unleashed exclaiming: *"de Gaulle is playing the game of a small minority of extremists who want the separation of Quebec."* (72% of French Canadians were favourable of the policies of de Gaulle: Four million... that makes a nice "small minority of extremists".)

As an interesting anecdote, Daniel Johnson succeeded, through the help of Pierre Laporte, in passing a surprising resolution in the Chamber: *"I would like to make a proposition, although it requires the unanimous consent of the Chamber, to thank General de Gaulle, for having come to Quebec on our invitation, and chastise the federal government that has ensured he not be able to finish his trip in Canada..."* [7]

It is quite interesting to note that René Lévesque, the Parti Québécois's future leader, one of the leaders of the real minority of separatists, was not at all happy with de Gaulle's move: *"We tried, until the last moment, to convince Aquin [one of Lévesque's colleague] not to go ahead with his statement [in favour of de Gaulle]. (...) It didn't take long before he was dubbed a Gaullist MNA. That's exactly what we wanted to avoid when forming the movement. (...) You will find it was one of the major reasons we delayed the creation of the movement."*

Showing a total lack of understanding towards de Gaulle's design, Lévesque continues: *"We maintain an enormous gratitude to de Gaulle, for having, by this happy mistake, made us known to the world."* Lévesque says "mistake", what a lack of insight! As if the British Empire's attack on de Gaulle was based on the *"Vive le Québec Libre"*... De Gaulle had put sticks in the Empire's gears the whole time he was President of the FrenchRepublic.

That is why they hated him so much, not for few words said on the balcony of Montreal's City Hall.

# CH. IV PART 3 - FREEDOM FOR THE WHOLE OF CANADA

De Gaulle was never a separatist. On the contrary, it could be said that he was more favourable to a Canadian marriage than a Quebec–British relationship. The official declaration of the French Ministers Council of July 31 1967 was clear: *"He (de Gaulle) was brought to measure their will (of the French Canadians) to attain the evolution that would need to be accomplished by Canada as a whole to control their own affairs and become masters of their own progress."*

Contrary to popular opinion, de Gaulle's intentions were never to destroy Canada, but rather to liberate it from the British octopus, so that all of Canada could enjoy the liberty that would be the effect of France's policy of Progress, Independence and Peace. While de Gaulle and Johnson clearly wanted to liberate Quebec, they knew that it wouldn't be possible as long as Canada were an appendage of the Crown... During his press conference of November 27, 1967 at the Palais de l'Elysée, de Gaulle explained what two "preconditions" were absolutely necessary for a "free Quebec" to come into being.

The first would be a "complete change of the Canadian political structure" that had been established a century earlier by the British Monarchy. The second condition would necessitate the re-uniting of lost bonds between the French cultures on both sides of the Atlantic in solidarity. Alas, today we know that a series of (well synchronized) heart attacks insured that the historic reunion that de Gaulle dreamed of would not occur. This failure contributed directly to the formation of the terrible Anglo–American geopolitical system that we know today.

## Diefenbaker, de Gaulle and Johnson

Throughout the 1960s, Daniel Johnson fought to ensure that not only Quebec, but Canada as a whole would eventually become sovereign and adopt a republican constitution. He understood, as General de Gaulle did also, that the proper development of a French society within Canada could only occur if Canada itself became a sovereign nation based upon a principle of progress. This is the only way to comprehend Johnson`s battle cry *"independence if necessary, but not necessarily independence"*.

This understanding was evidenced in Johnson's energetic support to ensure the sweeping victory of John Diefenbaker as Prime Minister in 1957 and 1958 winning the full support of the Union Nationale. Diefenbaker is distinguished as the only Canadian Prime Minister to campaign vigorously for a full Canadian development plan and devotion to scientific and technological progress, going so far as to fight for the establishment of a Canadian Credit System for the first (and only) time in history [8]. To the astonishment of all, Diefenbaker's Conservatives swept the elections taking even the majority of the vote in Quebec, a province which had never broken with its support of the federal Liberal Party since the days of Wilfrid Laurier. Since their original meeting in a Commonwealth Conference of Parliamentarians in 1950, Diefenbaker and Johnson would be allies with Johnson even being considered *"the right arm of Diefenbaker in Quebec"*. [9]

Diefenbaker was also known to be allied closely with General de Gaulle during this period. This friendship quickly formed after their first 1958 meeting in Paris. Years later, Diefenbaker would write of his friendship with de Gaulle in the following terms: *"I was very much impressed with de Gaulle's wisdom and with the fullness of his dedication to the service of France. In truth, he was the soul of France... Of all the official visits that I made during my period of office, none exceeded in splendour General de Gaulle's reception in honour of Canada."*[10]

The admiration both leaders shared for one another established a foundation of cooperation based upon a common recognition that the sovereignty of nations rested upon their commitment to constant rejuvenation. Were the policies of Diefenbaker and his "Northern Vision" to succeed, a systemic overhaul of the Canadian federal political structure must necessarily have occurred. A universal cultural heritage of progress would have established a principle upon which a multi linguistic unified country of various ethnicities could organically be nourished and grow. Without this orientation and a unified sense of national mission living in the hearts of a people, any nation were doomed to division, and multicultural stagnation under the Social Darwinist laws of "each against all". Both de Gaulle and Johnson were undoubtedly sensitive to this fact, although Diefenbaker the unrepentant monarchist was somewhat more naïve regarding the obstacles that would be set in his path and eventually sabotage much of his attempted revolution in physical economics and statecraft.

During his Ottawa message of April 18 1960, Charles de Gaulle expressed his feeling of a Canada pregnant with the potential for progressive change, in the following terms:

*"How delighted and honoured I am to find myself on Canadian soil. Many are the reasons for this: first of all, our deeply rooted past- numerous indeed are the*

*links which bound us, and which, indeed, still bind us- and then there is the more recent past. I recall the two World Wars in which your country and mine joined forces in the battle for freedom of the world... I am therefore pleased to be back on your soil, and to renew my many friendships, and to greet you in the name of France. Long live Canada, Long live France, and Long live the free peoples!"*

# From a British to an American Constitution

While often critical of the direction America had chosen to pursue in the post-Kennedy era, de Gaulle and Johnson were not at all opposed to the United States as a country; that is to say, the essence and soul of the United States expressed in its constitution. This fact is evidenced by Daniel Johnson's constitution project where on page 19 of his *Égalité ou Indépendance*, we can read: ***"It were wise to examine what opportunities exist to replace the British based parliamentary system with a congressional system based upon the American model"***.

The problem is clear. The origin of those terrible things which we here in Canada have often attributed to the "American Empire" can usually be traced back to an oligarchy in the City of London, moving quietly through networks in the Canadian Establishment. De Gaulle, who had access to the most efficient intelligence services of the day, would certainly not ignore the evil role played by the secret societies and elite clubs loyal to the Empire. Those networks, which had come to determine in large part United States foreign policy, have had the tendency to induce the USA to behave very much contrary to its historical nature. On top of that, these networks are highly ingrained and protected throughout Canada.

By the beginning of the 1960s, the world was entering a very unstable period. The fruits of those great works planted by de Gaulle over the years following WW II, would reveal a new dimension to the French identity centered on "progress, independence and peace", and come to play a crucial role in history. Under de Gaulle's leadership, a new era was taking form: He would remove all French forces from NATO, he refused England's desired entry into the Common Market since he knew that if they would be permitted entrance, then his Grand Design of a Europe as agreed upon by himself and Germany's Chancellor Konrad Adenauer, from "the Atlantic to the Urals" could never come into existence. De Gaulle wanted a "détente", and that would involve ending the cold war, and advancing policies of economic cooperation between the East and West. This period therefore elicited great hope among republican forces.

# CH. IV PART 4 – DANIEL JOHNSON'S COURAGE

At the official dinner honouring General de Gaulle on the evening of his arrival in Québec, Daniel Johnson was full of hope and outlined his acceptance of the General's challenge to join in his Great Design.

*"Under your leadership, France has recovered a stability that merits our admiration. She has vigorously pursued a vast program of national planning which, in two decades, has justified your unshakable faith in what you yourself have called the 'genius of rebirth."*

*"[...] but your light shines beyond the frontiers of old Europe as witnessed by the eloquent receptions of which you were the object in Asia and in the Americas during recent years. Your understanding of world problems, your decisiveness and your tenacity executing your ideas polarizes the hopes of numerous countries. Your diplomatic actions have proven in many ways to be one of the most powerful factors of international equilibrium."*

Two days later, just before de Gaulle's departure, Johnson added that he believed a new era was opening up for Quebec on the world stage, and that Quebec would be able to play a role of partner and unifying force to achieve universal good will. In the mind of the Premier, the French nation in America would enter world history and realize her international role.

Upon returning to Paris, de Gaulle explained his political vision to the French people, a vision which Anglo American political forces acting through the French press and political channels rabidly attacked. In his televised address of August 10, 1967, the General demonstrated that the liberation of "New France" was a necessary aspect of French foreign policy.

*"Ordinarily, each of us- and this is very normal- is absorbed by the circumstances and demands of daily life and thus takes very little time to look at the whole of which they are a part, or what could become of our country. And yet, everything depends upon it [...]. As in the tense situation in which the world finds itself, our peoples' actions weigh heavily on her destiny. We have the opportunity today to ask what goals are necessary for the direction of the country and which path will best achieve them?*

*[...] Progress, independence and peace, are those goals which our political decisions must follow [...] In this way, all that is realized in the development of the country, in whatever domain, at whatever moment, in any way, is fought in principle and without exception, all of the time, by those humble followers of its truth. The fact that France, without denying any friendship to Anglo American nations, but breaking with absurd conformity and outdated habits, takes a proper French position on the subject of the war in Viet Nam and the conflict in the Middle East, or- no later than yesterday- of the unanimous and powerful will to franchise that French Canadians manifested around the President of the French Republic, stupefied and indignant as they were to the apostles of decline."*

# Conclusion

For over four decades, a blinding darkness has spread across the Quebec political scene. After the death of Daniel Johnson, the nightmarish vision of those "apostles of decline" began to be felt across all of Canada. Over the recent decades, no one has yet risen to shine light on the road to progress, as the light of Johnson's spirit was no longer directly visible. The English and French populations of Canada had fallen as moths at night, upon the blinding flame of the Empire, with Canadian Prime Minister Pierre Elliot Trudeau on one side, and his counterweight, René Lévesque on the other. Canadians thought they had to pick either one of the two, without ever considering for one instant that either choice would have them fall under a single trap.

Would it not have been better to return to a saner period of our history and to follow the example of those individuals who understood those goals of Progress, Development, Cooperation and Peace? Why must we continue to admire those who, consciously or not, brought the vision of de Gaulle and Johnson to ruin? Why must we continuously give our admiration to those who resisted joining their efforts when the time was ripe? Whether you were for or against René Lévesque is not important, but the great error of those living at that time, was their belief that René Lévesque truly desired independence and sovereignty, or even that Lévesque represented, under one form or another, the continuity of the "de Gaulle-Johnson" tradition.

Johnson's presentation of his project for a constitutional republic to liberate all of Canada, and as de Gaulle hoped, transform the soul of the United States at the same time, was one of the most dangerous moments in the Empire's recent history.

By the end of the 1960s, the choking of the "French effort" had become a terrible success, culminating with the death of Johnson, the fall of de Gaulle in France the following year, and the October crisis of 1970. The later October Crisis was an operation directed by the Special services of Anglo American interests, which terrorized hundreds of thousands of Quebecois under the dynamic of terrorism, cultural irrationalism and martial law, to the point that the traumatized population forgot what exactly de Gaulle and Johnson were trying to do for them. Little by little, the consolidation of perfidious independence movements, of which René Lévesque was a key figurehead, became hegemonic and a trap for those in whose hearts a flame of liberty had not yet been extinguished.

It is never easy to admit to have been scammed, especially when that scam, under various guises, spanned a period of over four decades. The majority of those members of the Parti Québécois or Bloc Québécois are not necessarily bad people, if perhaps a little naïve. In general most people who want sovereign change have a positive inclination and disgust for the effects of imperialism, but the fact of being emotionally attached to false institutions and false axioms that have led directly to civilization's enslavement and downfall, will forever keep them from representing the true interests of our people.

# CHAPTER V – THE FIGHT FOR CONTINENTAL WATER MANAGEMENT IN QUEBEC

While minister of Hydraulic Resources under the leadership of l'Union Nationale Premier Maurice Duplessis (1945-1959), Daniel Johnson championed large scale water and hydroelectric projects, making Quebec into the premier pioneer of hydroelectric engineering in the world. Prior to Maurice Duplessis, Québec's break with cultural backwardness that had plagued its population for so long, had been initiated most boldly with Premier Adélard Godbout (1939-1944) and his creation of Hydro Quebec via the nationalization of Montreal Light, Heat and Power Company. Godbout's collaborator Louis Philippe Pigeon was inspired by Roosevelt's Tennessee Valley Authority, and began bold programs that unleashed cheap electricity, advanced agricultural technologies and rural electrification, breaking the usurious private stranglehold of Montreal Light, Heat and Power which had been prohibiting development and squeezing the population dry with expensive and unreliable electricity for decades.

By 1959, approximately half of Canada's hydroelectric power was coming from Quebec, and a culture of progress was finally beginning to blossom through the aid of the unique `Classical education` system whose design was to create morally developed citizens fluent in classical literature, as well as Greek and Latin.

After Duplessis` untimely death in 1959, the next wave of cleansing of radically regressive elements inside of the Quebec establishment occurred during the "100 day revolution" of Paul Sauvé, Duplessis' successor. Under Premier Sauvé and Johnson, the trans-Canada highway was constructed through Quebec, and an array of social reforms were implemented leading to increased funding to classical colleges and increased minimum wages. Johnson was also given carte blanche to use Quebec-based engineers instead of Duplessis' intention to use only American firms to construct Quebec's energy and water development projects.

Daniel Johnson would lead in the initiation of several ambitious hydroelectric programs during the last years of the 1950s which would include the Manicouagan 1, 2, 3 and 5 as well as three sites at the Outardes River with the 2600 Megawatt (MW) Manicouagan 5, or "Manic 5" dam as the largest of the set. The Dams would impound the world's fifth largest asteroid impact crater creating the fifth largest reservoir in the world. The total electricity development of these projects would be over 7500MW! The real wealth however, would be located not in the increased electricity, monetary profits or even productivity of the society, but rather in the intellectual and cultural revolution that would transform a submissive society into proud citizens due to their increased mastery of nature. The former boundary conditions that had held Quebec back in a closed system and a logic of scarcity, were being quickly eliminated to the horror of the British Empire.

# The Quiet Counter-Revolution

After untimely heart attacks killed both Maurice Duplessis in 1959 and his successor Paul Sauvé four months later, the Union Nationale fizzled out and was replaced by the "new reformers" of the Liberal Party of Jean Lesage and a clique of authors largely run out of the University of Laval, of a program later called "The Quiet Revolution". This program was led by René Lévesque who became Minister of Natural Resources, a disciple of Father George Henri Lévesque named Maurice Lamontagne, and a young Rhodes Scholar named Paul Gérin-Lajoie. These characters had spearheaded the establishment of the first Ministry of Education, cleansing the educational system of all traces of classical-humanism. While Lévesque went on to form the Parti Québécois (PQ) 16 days after Johnson's death, Maurice Lamontagne became an influential Senator and Chair of the Commission which purged Canadian science policy in 1970 bringing in the Organization for Economic Cooperation and Development's (OECD's) Systems Analysis. This strategy was being led at the time by Alexander King, then science director of the OECD, and later co-founder of the Malthusian Club of Rome, whose Canadian branch included Maurice Lamontagne as a founding member. In 1970, Gérin-Lajoie would head up the Canadian International Development Agency (CIDA) created by Maurice Strong two years earlier.

Gérin-Lajoie employed his fellow Rhodes Scholar Jean Beetz to direct the Institute for Research into Public Law (IRPL) at the Université Laval in 1961, providing Pierre Trudeau with his first teaching position after having been blacklisted by Duplessis for years. This institute also brought Trudeau's inner circle collaborators Marc Lalonde and Michael Pitfield in on the Board of Directors. All of these "new reformers" were united in having come to prominence writing for the influential anti-Duplessis magazine Cité Libre, begun by Trudeau in 1950. At this time Pitfield and Lalonde were busily working as assistants to Federal Minister of Justice Davie Fulton whose assignment was to sabotage the design of W.A.C. Bennett's "Two Rivers" development policy in British Columbia [1]. Fulton was also a Rhodes Scholar and was allied with another "new nationalist" named General Andrew McNaughton, then Canadian head of the International Joint Commission charged with overseeing transboundary water issues with the United States. Their chosen method of proposing water projects on the West Coast that would cut off the Americans and direct water to Canadians only, would be attempted in the East Coast as well as we shall soon see. The fear of "continentalism" driven by technological progress and joint development of resources amongst Canada and the USA was the greatest motivator of the British Empire at this time.

While many elements intent on bringing in "scientific" (aka: system's analysis) methods of management in political and educational planning were introduced with these Liberals, positive elements such as Adélard Godbout's old ally Louis-Philippe Pigeon was brought in to help plan for Quebec's development as well. Daniel Johnson's friend Pierre Laporte also became a leader within the "new reformers" and went on to be assassinated by the RCMP controlled FLQ terrorist cells in October 1970. Some of these elements, including Jean Lesage himself, would became influenced by the aggressive diplomacy of Charles de Gaulle who intended for Quebec to take on a key role in his international "Grand Design".

Johnson's plans for the Manicouagan and Outardes dams were almost thwarted early on due to the intervention by Lord Edmund Leopold de Rothschild who commissioned a study to exploit the 5428 MW hydro potential of Labrador's Churchill Falls as an alternative to moving ahead with the Johnson design. General McNaughton became an avid champion of the Rothschild project and had it gone through then no culture of Quebec engineering or development would have occurred as it did, and a greater degree of separation of Canada from the USA would have been effected.

Through the influence of Johnson's allies in the Liberal Party, as well as Charles de Gaulle's advice, Lesage was swayed to break with the Rothschild policy and moved ahead with the Johnson plan employing Quebec engineers. By 1965 Lesage became even more uncooperative with the British-run `New Reformers` when he rejected his former adherence to the `Fulton-Favreau` formula for constitutional reform then being pushed by Gérin-Lajoie and the IRPL. A \$100 million loan provided by B.C.'s Premier W.A.C. Bennett who was busy fighting a similar battle on the West Coast was also used to help Jean Lesage access highly needed capital to begin construction of the Manicouagan and Outardes dams.

The intention to keep society stuck within frameworks of fixed parameters, both materially and intellectually, has been the driver of this past cycle of history that began with the deaths of Paul Sauvé, and John F. Kennedy. The fact that mankind`s relationship with the biosphere is not fixed, but rather dynamic has been a troublesome reality which those self-proclaimed `gods` and their lackeys would try desperately to conceal.

The sole metric of value worth anything must be founded on the fact that the biosphere`s evolution is the effect of an anti-entropic directionality underlying the fabric of the universe, and when humanity abides by its own anti-entropic potential by making ever more advanced discoveries into the universe, those parameters defining his limits melt away and ever greater states of freedom are opened to his potential sphere of activity. By disregarding this fact, the British Empire, and all empires necessarily force themselves into the conclusion, as Aeschylus`s Zeus had done, that depopulation and the management of diminishing resources is the unfortunate basis upon which its continued existence must be maintained.

Let us learn from the lesson of Charles de Gaulle, Paul Sauvé and Daniel Johnson by throwing off the shackles of Zeus and return to a spirit of progress before the path towards a new dark age becomes one from which we can no longer return.

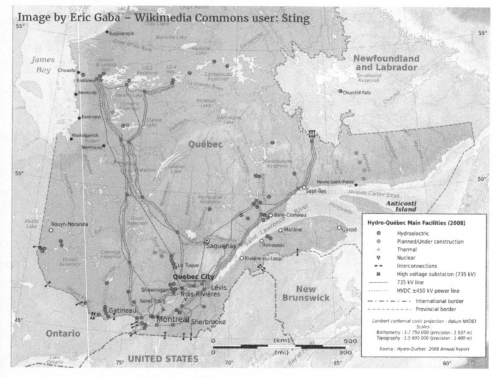

Above: Quebec's Hydropower infrastructure would not exist were it not for the pioneering spirit of Adelair Godbout, and the Union Nationale government led by Paul Sauve, Maurice Duplessis and especially Daniel Johnson Sr.
Below: The Manicouagan-5 Dam (AKA: the Daniel Johnson Dam) which was the world's largest Multi arch buttress dam. Premier Johnson was found dead the morning he was scheduled to give the inaugural speech at the opening of the project.

# The Forgotten Nation builders of Quebec

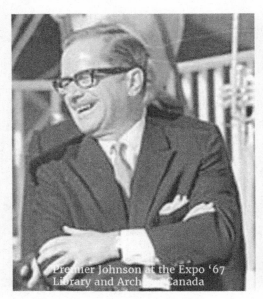

Premier Johnson at the Expo '67
Library and Archives Canada

Quebec nation builders who brought French Canada out of the dark age of ignorance
included such pioneers as Union Nationale's Daniel Johnson Sr (above left),
Liberal Primier during WW2 Adelard Godbout (above right), Premier Maurice
Duplessis (bottom left), Premier Paul Sauve (bottom middle), and Premier
Jean Lesage (bottom right) who broke with the technocrats running the Quiet
Revolution and attempted to revive the C.D. Howe Liberal agenda by collaborating
with Johnson's agenda for development

# CHAPTER VI – THE UGLY TRUTH OF GENERAL MACNAUGHTON BY RICHARD SANDERS

*The following chapter was written by American scholar Richard Sanders and serves as an important addition to the Untold History of Canada.*

Just mention the word "Dieppe" around older Canadians and you'll be stirring up a hornet's nest. The Dieppe raid was the worst disaster in Canadian military history; and everybody involved tries to pass the buck; but the real truth is that it was not an accident, but deliberate – and that buck stops with Churchill, Lord Mountbatten and, specifically, General Andrew McNaughton, the same McNaughton who designed and ran the hated 'relief camps' during the Depression.

Dieppe, August 19, 1942, 0500h. Landing craft filled with about 50 U.S. Army Rangers, 1000 British troops, and 5000 Canadian soldiers are behind schedule. At 0507h the sun comes up, the first craft still 30 meters off shore and the Germans begin firing, shooting them like fish in a barrel.

In a retrospective article of Nov. 8, 2012, the grandson of Captain L.G. Alexander, a Calgary doctor and medical officer for the 14th Canadian Army Tank Regiment (Calgary Regiment) who survived,  writes in the Rocky Mountain Outlook of Banff, Alberta:

"*Our boat was now [about 9 am] hopeless,*" Alexander wrote of LCT 8. "All the Naval crew were either killed or blown overboard and we floated sideways into the Beach, receiving broadsides from all of the shore guns. Machine gun bullets were beating a constant tattoo on the boat. Explosions were occurring inside and out, and at one time the inside of the boat was a sheet of flame.

"*Men were blown overboard, many of whom I had just finished bandaging when I turned back I found had been killed, and nearly all were blown completely off the ship ... By now, of the 130 men who set out on LCT 8 the day before, 97 had been killed, wounded or captured. The smokestack and bridge of LCT 8 had been blown away. The hull was riddled with holes, both numerous small ones and 32 larger ones caused by shelling."*

The British provided very little air support for the infantrymen trying to land, ostensibly for fear of causing too many civilian casualties! The naval bombardment from British ships amounted to mere pin pricks; the Germans were fighting from fortified strong points so that hundreds of the assault troops never made it off the beaches, and within a few hours, nearly 2000 were forced to surrender. The Churchill tanks that were supposed to support the infantry immediately got mired down in the pebbles on the steep beaches, and every single one of them was destroyed.

Who was responsible for this disaster? Even General Montgomery had wanted to scrub the plan after the original date of July 4 had to be postponed because of bad weather:

*"[Once the original plan was postponed] ...it was reasonable to expect that it was now a common subject of conversation in billets and pubs in the south of England, since nearly 5000 Canadian soldiers were involved as well as considerable numbers of sailors and airmen. ... But Combined Operations Headquarters thought otherwise; they decided to revive it and got the scheme approved by the British Chiefs of Staff towards the end of July. When I heard of this I was very upset; I considered that it would no longer be possible to maintain secrecy. Accordingly I wrote to General Paget, C.-in-C. Home Forces, telling him of my anxiety, and recommending that the raid on Dieppe should be considered cancelled "for all time." If it was considered desirable to raid the Continent, then the objective should not be Dieppe. This advice was disregarded. On the 10th August I left England to take command of the Eighth Army in the desert." [1]*

Clearly, Churchill's hand-picked 'Adviser on Combined Operations' Commodore Lord Louis Mountbatten had no such qualms. As for General McNaughton, he had been working hand-in-glove with the British

Commander in Chief Home Forces, General Paget, in planning an "expeditionary force" which was to be under Paget's direction...

*"Paget said that it was now intended to set up an Expeditionary Force Planning Staff Committee, and that this would be composed of himself as chairman, Admiral Sir Bertram Ramsay (C.-in-C. Dover) as Naval representative, Air Chief Marshal Sir Sholto Douglas (C.-in-C. Fighter Command) as Air representative, Major-General Chaney (Commanding General, United States Forces in the United Kingdom) to represent the United States, and General McNaughton to represent Canada."* [2]

McNaughton apparently continued to promote the Dieppe raid, even after General Montgomery had so strenuously objected. What kind of incompetence or malevolence would send these boys on this suicide mission? The Germans clearly had time to catch wind of the intended "surprise" and prepare themselves; they had even spotted concentrations of landing craft in British harbors and had attacked some of them!

But the many warning signs were unheeded. The net result: out of the 4,963 Canadians who had sailed from England early that morning, 907 were killed, and 2460 were wounded or taken prisoner – a 68 percent casualty rate [3]... all within six hours. There is no record that McNaughton, who was supposed to represent the Canadians, ever tried to stop it. Why were the Canadians chosen as cannon fodder? The British have the reputation of letting the colonials do the fighting for them. Churchill feared that the world was catching on to this: *"I am grieved at [the] Australian attitude, but I have long feared the dangerous reactions on Australian and world opinion of our seeming to fight all our battles in the Middle East only with Dominion troops."* [4]

The Dieppe disaster certainly served the British Empire! By late 1941 and early 1942, the Russians and the US were insisting on the need to open a second front to defeat Nazi Germany. But Churchill, more interested in preserving the Empire than winning the war, wanted to convince Stalin and Roosevelt that a landing in Europe was infeasible "this early," – so Churchill needed a clamorous failure, – and got one.

# Flashback to the Depression: McNaughton's Royal Twenty Center camps [3]

Given McNaughton's pre-war record, could the English King George have expected any lesser service to the Empire? The response of the Roosevelt administration to the Depression was to organize huge infrastructural development programs to immediately begin a recovery of the productive civilian economy. The Works Progress Administration (WPA), Peoples Work Administration (PWA) and the Civilian Conservation Corps (CCC) provided on-the-job training, education, and productive work at reasonable wages — the CCC (1933-1943) being especially popular, with men riding the rails or walking thousands of miles to become part of this. Octogenarians would point out to their great grandchildren: "I built this." Major General Andrew McNaughton, the army chief of staff, did the diametric opposite. His biography describes his response to the Depression, honeyed o'er with McNaughton's own words: *"to proceed by persuasion and not by compulsion, and to do everything possible to facilitate the flow of men back to industry..."* [4] – but it amounted to a failure to deal with the underlying problem of an unproductive economy, and rather to contain potential trouble by military means. The relief camps were proposed by McNaughton, and Prime Minister R.B. Bennett chose him to run them. Young people in the American CCC camps lived in decent conditions, were paid a dollar a day and performed work such as planting trees and building state park recreational facilities which are part of the general welfare; the young Canadians in the relief camps were paid a miserable $.20 a day and lived in tarpaper shacks. Soon they smelled more like Hitler's camps, and McNaughton used this almost "free" labor for a large number of military projects. [5]

Resistance to the camps was enormous and almost universal. Strike after strike was called, and a peaceful march on Ottawa was stopped in June of 1935 in Regina, Saskatchewan when on Ottawa orders, the (federal) Royal Canadian Mounted Police began clubbing unarmed marchers and ordinary citizens indiscriminately, injuring hundreds of residents and marchers; one marcher was killed and it might have ended in a massacre had the provincial government not pressured Ottawa to call off their police. [6]

The camps and other policies of the sitting government were so unpopular that in the 1935 election, the ruling Conservative Party dropped from 134 to 39 seats; in 1936, the new government of MacKenzie King shut down the camps.

# McNaughton's Sabotage of NAWAPA

The British hated President Kennedy, his brother Robert, W.A.C. Bennett, for their promotion of continental planning of water management which had culminated in the Great North American Water and Power Alliance.

The British hated NAWAPA because continental water management would mean that the whole continent would slip out of their grasp, along with their hope of bringing the USA back into the imperial fold. NAWAPA had enormous support all over Canada [7]; for example, in 1965, Prime

Minister Lester Pearson purged two anti-NAWAPA ministers from his cabinet – and the future looked very promising. So the British deployed McNaughton, who had expertise on water issues through his work as the Canadian head of the International Joint Commission (IJC). The General spent the last years of his life fighting NAWAPA tooth and nail.

McNaughton gave three speeches to the ruling elites of Canada, one of them in the form of a debate against Senator Frank Moss of Utah, the international champion of NAWAPA. McNaughton called the Columbia River treaty "pillage" by the US, called NAWAPA a "monstrous concept," based upon "a diabolic thesis that all waters of North America become a shared resource" all to make *existing desert areas ... bloom at the expense of development in Canada.*" [8] A cynical manipulation. Managing the continental watershed, and harnessing the enormous hydroelectric power, and the benefits of irrigation and highly-improved infrastructure and transportation would have been, and will be, of incalculable benefit for Canada, the US and Mexico alike; but not to the benefit of the British Empire. You might say in a nutshell, that McNaughton fought to deny Americans and Mexicans access to fresh water currently being dumped into the salt ocean, just in case the Empire might some day in the unforeseeable future, need that water to wash the Queen's dirty laundry.

# THE MURDER OF JFK

Two of McNaughton's key allies in the fight to thwart the design of B.C. Premier W.A.C. Bennett's design for the Columbia River Treaty and Peace River projects were two lawyers steered directly by the upper echelons of British intelligence: Davie Fulton and Maj. Louis Mortimer Bloomfield. Fulton was a young Oxford Rhodes scholar working as Justice Minister in

Ottawa under Diefenbaker, who openly tried to sabotage Bennett's proposals for a two basin policy in tandem with the Columbia River Treaty. This Bennett design provided a direct outline of what was to become the NAWAPA design later. Fulton fought to support the McNaughton alternative design which involved bringing the Canadian water flows into the Prairies and letting the Americans hang out to dry.

Major Bloomfield, then head of the Permindex assassination cabal [outlined in the accompanying study on p. 38] was close friends with both Fulton and McNaughton. Working directly under McNaughton at the IJC in 1958, Bloomfield authored "Boundary Water Problems of Canada and the United States" which produced a legal case against W.A.C. Bennett and Frank Moss's approach to continental water management. Fulton would happily describe Bloomfield as his "dear friend" after a Conservative Party convention in 1967. [9]

Gen. Andrew MacNaughton (left–
National Archives of Canada)

Above: His associate and fellow British
agent Maj. Louis Mortimer Bloomfield

Below: Canadian bodies litered on the
ground during the infamous Dieppe Raid.

Leading advocates of NAWAPA and continental
water management during the 1960s included
B.C. Premier W.A.C. Bennett (below), President
John F. Kennedy (bottom right), Sen. Robert
Kennedy (right), and Sen. Frank Moss (top
right). It is no coincidence that the same
aparatus which orchestrated John F. Kennedy
was also aligned with the killing of NAWAPA.

# CHAPTER VII – MAURICE STRONG AND THE IMPERIAL ATTACK ON ATOMIC ENERGY

*"Isn't the only hope for the planet that the industrialized civilizations collapse? Isn't it our responsibility to bring that about?"*

*– Maurice Strong*

A nother leading figure in the Anglo-Dutch financial oligarchy's tool box of sociopathic agents is a Canadian-born operative by the name of Maurice Strong (1929-1915). Much has been written on Strong's role as a recruit of Rockefeller assets in the 1950s, an oil baron, vice president of Power Corporation by 30, Liberal Party controller, Privy Councilor, and founder of Canada's neo-colonial external aid policy towards Africa. I wish to draw your attention in this chapter on the role Strong has played since 1968 in subverting the anti-entropic potential of Canada and the world at large. It was through this post-1968 role that Strong performed his most valued work for the genocidal agenda of his British masters who seek to reduce the world population to a "carrying capacity" of less than a billion.

## RIO and Global Governance

In 1992, Maurice Strong had been assigned to head the second Earth Summit (the first having been the 1972 Stockholm Conference on the Human Environment also chaired by Strong). The Rio Summit had established a new era in the consolidation of NGOs and corporations under the genocidal green agenda of controlled starvation masquerading behind the dogma of "sustainability'. This doctrine was formalized with Agenda 21 and the Earth Charter, co-authored by Mikhail Gorbachev, Jim MacNeill and Strong. At the opening of the Rio Summit, Strong announced that industrialized countries had "developed and benefited from the unsustainable patterns of production and consumption which have produced our present dilemma. It is clear that current lifestyles and consumption patterns of the affluent middle class, involving high meat intake, consumption of large amounts of frozen and convenience foods, use of fossil fuels, appliances, home and work-place air-conditioning, and suburban housing- are not sustainable. A shift is necessary toward lifestyles less geared to environmentally damaging consumption patterns."

In a 1992 essay entitled *From Stockholm to Rio: A Journey Down a Generation*, published by the UN Conference on Environment and Development, Strong wrote:

*"The concept of national sovereignty has been an immutable, indeed sacred, principle of international relations. It is a principle which will yield only slowly and reluctantly to the new imperatives of global environmental cooperation. What is needed is recognition of the reality that in so many fields, and this is particularly true of environmental issues, it is simply not feasible for sovereignty to be exercised unilaterally by individual nation-states, however powerful. The global community must be assured of environmental security."*

# The Destruction of Nuclear Power

It is vital to examine Strong's role in destroying Canada's nuclear potential, one of the greatest beacons of hope mankind has ever had to break out of the current "fixed" boundaries to humanity's development. Indeed, the controlled use of the atom and the necessary discovery of new universal principles associated with this endeavour has always represented one of the greatest strategic threats to the oligarchic system which depends on a closed system of fixed resources in order to both manage current populations and justify global governance under "objective" frameworks of logic. Fission and fusion processes exist on a level far outside those fixed parameters that assume the earth's "carrying capacity" is no greater than 2 billion souls. If mankind were to recognize his unique creative potential to continuously transcend his limitations by discovering and creating new resources, no empire could long exist. With Canada as the second nation to have civilian nuclear power, and a frontier science culture in physics and chemistry, the need to destroy this potential in the mind of the proprietors of Canada was great indeed.

To get a better sense of the anti-nuclear role Strong has played in Canadian science policy, we must actually go back once again to Strong's reign at the Department of External Aid in 1966.

# Technological Apartheid for Africa

A key reason that Strong had been brought into Canada's Civil Service to head up the External Aid office in 1966 was to sabotage the international efforts leading scientists and statesmen had achieved in making Canada an exporter of its original CANDU reactors. Since 1955, leading patriots within Atomic Energy Canada Ltd. (AECL) and the National Research Council such as C.D. Howe and his collaborator C.W. Mackenzie, the exporting of nuclear power technology was made available to developing countries such as India and Pakistan. This policy was advanced vigorously by Prime Minister John Diefenbaker who also saw atomic power as the key to world peace.

The banners under which this advanced technology transfer occurred was both the Columbo Plan and President Dwight Eisenhower's Atoms for Peace. This progressive approach to international development defined "external aid" not around IMF conditionalities, or simply money for its own sake, but rather as the transfer of the most advanced science and technology to poor countries with the explicit intention that all nations would attain true sovereignty.

When Strong got to work in External Aid, and later formed Canadian International Development Agency, Canada's relationship to "LDCs" (lesser developed countries) became reduced to advancing "appropriate technologies" under the framework of monetarism and systems analysis. No technology or advanced infrastructure policy necessary for the independence of former colonies were permitted under this precursor to what later became known as "sustainability" and "zero growth". Under Strong's influence, Canada's role became perverted into inducing LDCs to become obedient to IMF "conditionalities" and the reforms of their bureaucracies demanded by the OECD in order to receive money. Both in Canada and in developing countries, Strong was among the key agents who oversaw the implementation of the OECD's strategy of "Systems Analysis" for national policy management.

# Petrol and Pandas

In his role as President of Petro Canada (1976-78), Strong endorsed the national call to create a nuclear moratorium for Canada which had been carried out by the Canadian Coalition for Nuclear Responsibility in 1977 [1]. This document not only demanded an immediate halt to the continuation of all reactors then under construction, but also made the sophistical argument that more jobs could be created if "ecologically friendly" energy sources and conservation methods were developed instead of nuclear and fossil fuels. Strange desires coming from an oil executive, but not so strange considering Strong's 1978-1981 role as Vice-President of the World Wildlife Fund (WWF), an organization founded by the British and Dutch monarchies as a Royal Dutch Shell initiative in 1961 [2]. Strong was Vice President during the same interval that WWF co-founder Prince Phillip was its President.

While still heading up the External Aid Department in 1967, Strong had been a founding member of the 1001 Club in 1971 which was an elite international organization created by Prince Bernhard of the Netherlands which was used to finance the emerging green agenda for world governance [see appendix]. The 1001 Club worked in tandem with Prince Bernhard's other secretive club known as the "Bilderberg Group" which he founded in 1954. In this position, Strong helped to recruit 80 Canadian "initiates" to this elite society otherwise known as "Strong's Kindergarden", the most prominent being Lord Conrad Black, Barrick Gold's Peter Munk and Permindex's late Sir Louis Mortimer Bloomfield. As documented elsewhere, the latter had been at the heart of the plot to assassinate President John F. Kennedy [3].

# Strong Decapitates Ontario Nuclear Energy

By 1992, Strong had completed his role heading the Rio Earth Summit in Brazil and had returned to his native land to attempt to finalize the dismantling of Canada's nuclear program in his new assignment as President of Ontario Hydro, a position he held from 1992 to 1995 under the formal invitation of Bob Rae, then-NDP Premier of Ontario and brother of Power Corp.'s John Rae. Bob Rae later served as the leader of the Liberal Party from 2011-2013 in preparation for Justin Trudeau's appointment to become the party's new figurehead in April of 2013. Bob Rae continues to serve as the true power behind the Liberal Party and a key handler of the party's figurehead Justin Trudeau.

With the most ambitious nuclear program in North America, Ontario was proving to be a thorn in the zero-growth agenda demanded by the British Empire when Strong was brought in. The completion of the massive Darlington system in Ontario had demonstrated what successful long term science planning could accomplish, although the utility found itself running far over budget. The budgetary problems occurring as they did during a deep recession in 1992 were used by Strong to "restructure" the provincial energy utility.

The "remedies" chosen by Strong to solve Ontario Hydro's financial woes involved the immediate cancellation of all new nuclear energy development then being planned, firing 8 of the 14 directors, and downsizing the utility by laying off 14 000 employees, many of whom being the most specialized and experienced nuclear technicians in Canada. To add insult to injury, Strong used $10 million dollars of Ontario taxpayer revenue to purchase 31 000 acres  of Costa Rican rain forest for Conservation with the justification being that the Peruvian trees would offset the carbon emissions produced by Ontario's coal plants in the fight against the non-existent global warming!

Before leaving his post in 1995 with the fall of Bob Rae's government, Strong ensured that his work would continue with his replacement Jim MacNeill who headed Ontario Hydro from 1994 to 1997. MacNeill was co-architect of both the Earth Charter and the genocidal Agenda 21 during the Rio Summit and a long time British agent. Under MacNeill, Strong's mandate to unnecessarily shut down eight reactors for refurbishment and one permanently was effected in 1997, while Ontario Hydro itself was broken up into three separate entities. With the irreparable loss of specialized manpower and skills Strong and MacNeill left Ontario Hydro and Atomic Energy Canada Ltd. (AECL) mortally wounded for years to come.

Surprising all observers, (including Maurice Strong), AECL and the Ontario utilities were able to remobilize their remaining forces to pull together the successful refurbishment of all reactors, the last of which came back online in October 2012 with plans for two more in the near future. Sadly, as of October 2013, both of those two plans have been cancelled.

Although the parts would slowly be pieced back together at Ontario's nuclear facilities, AECL did not recover from this onslaught. The damage inflicted by Strong and MacNeill resulted in AECL's full privatization under Prime Minister Stephen Harper in 2011. AECL, a crown corporation created by "Minister of Everything" C.D. Howe in 1952 to oversee all CANDU reactor development was sold for the bargain basement price of $15 million to SNC-Lavalin without any plans for new research or even forward thinking projects and its future remains in question.

# Strong's Asian Infiltration

Before his death in 2015, Strong's talents were put to use in failed efforts to subvert Asian development. He was positioned in Beijing University as an Honorary Professor and Chairman of its Environmental Foundation and Chairman of the Advisory Board of the Institute for Research on Security and Sustainability for Northwest Asia.

In the face of the meltdown of the Trans-Atlantic economy, the Chinese have valiantly resisted pressure to succumb to the Green Agenda, submit their national sovereignty to the "New World Order" of zero-growth and depopulation. In spite of this pressure, a powerful tradition of

Confucianism and its commitment to progress has demonstrated its powerful influence in the various branches of the Chinese establishment who see China's only hope to survive located in its strategic partnership with Russia and long term megaprojects to lift its people out of poverty and into the 22nd Century.

Not only that, but the rejection of all "bottom up" NGO approaches to governance has also been vital for China's capacity to stabilize its nation and advance top down projects such as the Yangtze Three Gorges Dam (completed in 2010), the Belt and Road Initiative, the "Move South Water North Project" now underway, advanced space exploration, lunar mining prospects and advanced nuclear power programs using the CANDU designs as well as advanced Fourth Generation Thorium Reactors.

With Chinese Premier Xi Jinping's strategy for a New Silk Road uniting the Eurasian Continent, a new great potential has expressed itself and the future-oriented outlook shared among other Shanghai Cooperation Organization nations are the keys to breaking off the reliance on diminishing raw materials and fossil fuels which are currently monopolized by the British Empire's networks globally.

Maurice Strong (pictured above) was not only a a founding member of Prince Philip's 1001 Club, but was also a Vice-President of the World Wildlife Foundation while the Prince (below left) was its president. Blow middle and right are Stong's Canadian associate Jim Macneil and a co-controller of the 1960s Liberal Party of Canada Walter Lockhart Gordon..

# CHAPTER VIII – A LOOK TO THE FUTURE: REVIVING THE SPIRIT OF OUR NATION BUILDERS

*In this last chapter, let us take the lessons of history and leap into the future. The spirit of those nation builders which have been too long buried have been given a chance at new life within the context of the newly emerging paradigm led by the BRICS and China's New Silk Road.*

# Planning the Present Starts from the FUTURE

In a strained world looming on the brink of collapse and thermonuclear war on the one hand, and a new paradigm of mutual development and peaceful co-existence on the other, Canada's close geographical relationship to both the United States and Russia provides an ideal opportunity to act as a bridge uniting two parts of the world around advanced scientific, cultural and nation building endeavors centering around such programs as space science, nuclear energy, and arctic development. The lynchpin for these programs cumulatively driven by the World Landbridge now expressing itself as China's "New Silk Road"/ "Belt and Road Initiative", remains a centuries-long program called the Bering Strait Rail Tunnel, has been heralded by Lyndon LaRouche for over three decades as beacon of hope for world peace.

What would accepting the Russia/China offer to build it entail for Canada? What will be reactivated within our nation building history which Canadians have forgotten during 40+ years of post-industrial rot?

First and foremost, this New Silk Road program would mean abandoning the post-industrial system that replaced the 1945-1971 policy scientific and technological growth. Since the "petro dollar" was created over 40 years ago, a speculative instability has grown within the entire world which has resulted in Canada's loss of its manufacturing sector, while the financial services industries have grown exponentially. Once productive sectors have been converted to low wage service sectors while cultural decay has grown to intolerable proportions resulting in an epidemic of drugs/opiods, suicide, depression and escapism into degenerate forms of entertainment.

The Bering Strait Development Corridor demands a systemic top down evaluation of Canada's potential, not merely as a resource exporter, but as a driver of fundamental scientific progress in order to increase the energy flux density of humanity as a whole. Our frontiers obviously are found by pressing on the boundaries of human knowledge, in the atomic field on the immeasurably small, and in the space field on the immeasurably large. Geographically, the boundaries determining the last frontiers of earth are established by the Arctic.

Before proceeding to the most optimal choices of least action pathways and projects available for Canada within the context of a new emerging paradigm, it is important to take a brief inventory of the nature of the physical economy that we are dealing with. On a geographic level, The layout of Canada's development has to take into account the three fundamental zones:

1) Urban- Industrial where 80% of our population is located

2) Rural to the end of the tree line in the mid-Canada corridor

3) Arctic where less than 1% of Canadians live

As the 2011 Lpac research report "Arctic development and self-developing systems" and accompanying video "Breaking the Ice on Arctic Development" makes clear: True nation building must begin with the most underdeveloped region as the driver (the Arctic), which will then permit the mobilization of resources in order to "leapfrog" older technologies towards the cutting edge high energy flux density.

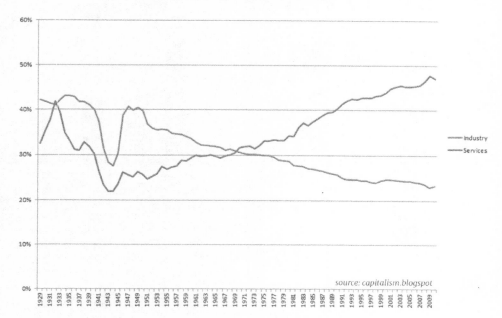

As an effect of the 1968-71 shift to a "post-industrial society", north america's labour force has been increasingly transformed into low wage service workers as evidenced by the graphs above and below. Meanwhile infrastructure has decayed through neglect, financial services exploded and Canada's reliance on revenues from resource extraction has grown cancerously large.

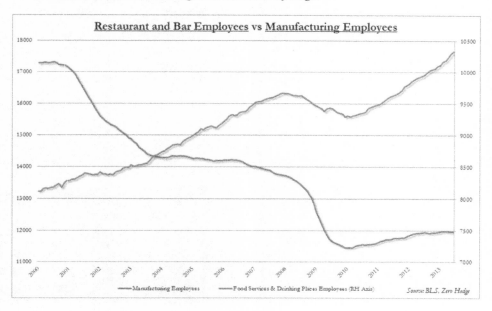

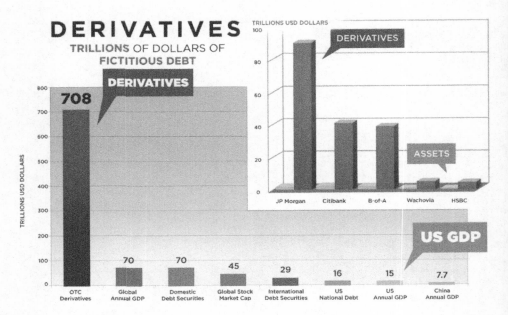

# DERIVATIVES
**TRILLIONS OF DOLLARS OF FICTITIOUS DEBT**

## The Cancer grows:

Above: the American derivatives growth compared to other variables in the world economy. These "creative financial instruments" have also taken over the 5 big Canadian banks featured below.

At right: LaRouche's triple curve showcases the nature of what a collapse function looks like with the bottom curve representing the physical (real) econoimc system while the upper two curves represent the purely financial. The start point is the 1971 de-coupling of the U.S dollar from the fixed exchange rate system.

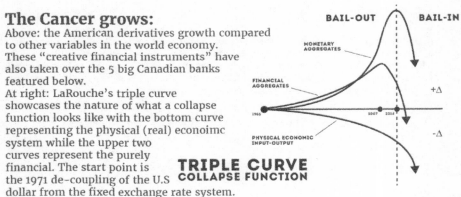

**TRIPLE CURVE COLLAPSE FUNCTION**

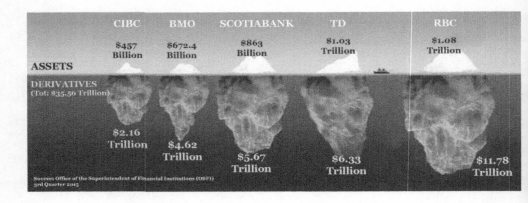

| | CIBC | BMO | SCOTIABANK | TD | RBC |
|---|---|---|---|---|---|
| **ASSETS** | $457 Billion | $672.4 Billion | $863 Billion | $1.03 Trillion | $1.08 Trillion |
| **DERIVATIVES** (Tot: $35.56 Trillion) | $2.16 Trillion | $4.62 Trillion | $5.67 Trillion | $6.33 Trillion | $11.78 Trillion |

Source: Office of the Superintendent of Financial Institutions (OSFI) 3rd Quarter 2015

# The Bering Strait Tunnel and Alaska–Canada Rail Corridor

The cornerstone of the World Landbridge, of which the Russian and Chinese led New Silk Road and New Trans-Eurasian development are vital components, is the construction of the Bering Strait Tunnel running from Russia to Alaska. Canada's vital contribution to this international project necessitates the completion of 1800 km of unbuilt rail, preferably high speed, from British Columbia, through the Yukon and into Alaska.

The Alaska-Canada rail connector, with the construction of a development corridor extending 80 km on each side of the railroad, can transform the region in its entirety. Power lines, fiber-optic lines, and where necessary, freshwater pipes would be encased within the corridor. Cities, population, manufacturing, and scientific agriculture would be fertilized and harvested in this corridor as well. The Arctic North's nearby abundant, but largely untapped, mineral and raw material resources would be made accessible, by rail link, out of the frigid ground for rational use in the Arctic North and the world.

This top down approach to rail creation sets the necessary foundation upon which any competent plan to reconstruct Canada's dilapidated municipal and interprovincial transportation infrastructure must rest. Magnetic Levitation trains connecting all major cities from Vancouver to the Maritimes would also provide a positive driver for nation building in tandem with a revived American and Mexican transportation strategy.

Were this program to be built, not only would countless productive jobs be created for the next generation, but a new breath of life for Canada and the world would result as an era of unbounded cooperation and creative discovery would necessarily result.

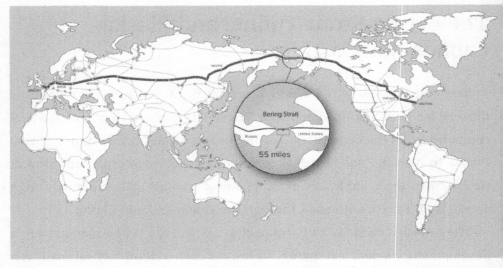

Above: The Bering Strait tunnel represents the keystone of the world landbridge

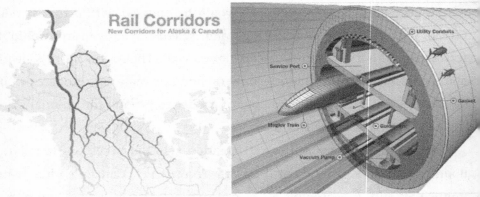

Above left and right: A closer view of of the rail network to be constructed as part of the Bering Strait project and a cutout of the underwater tunnel featuring pipelines, trains, and telecommunicatio

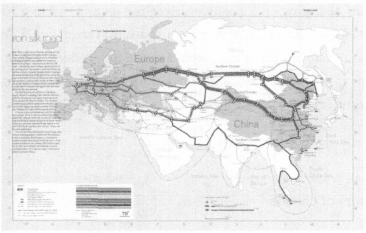

At left: An image of the major rail development corridors making up the New Silk Road

# Arctic Development

Ultimately, the opening up of the Arctic as the new frontier of human development requires that Canada learn from Russia's current commitment to build the new nuclear powered domed city of Umka on the island of Kotelny only 1000 km from the North Pole. In order to meet the challenge of housing over 5000 workers and their families in the harsh arctic climate which requires internal climate control, waste evaporation, internal agricultural capacities and reliable energy, Russian designers have used the International Space as their model. This ISS design is important since the Arctic will play a vital role in the investigation of cosmic radiation, a galactic (and intergalactic) phenomenon driving both the evolution of the living and non-living material on the earth.

This model "city of the future" echoes back to the planned domed city of Frobisher Bay, Nunavut which Prime Minister John Diefenbaker had committed to build as an integral component of his 1958 "Northern Vision" campaign. Frobisher Bay's design as produced by the Department of Public Works announced a domed city, encircled by 12 large towers housing 4500 workers and families connected by an underground network of tunnels. In order to ensure that this city were truly one of the future, recreation facilities, shopping centers and other amenities were included to ensure that the comfort of Toronto would be something accessible even in the Arctic.

Ultimately, Diefenbaker's Northern Vision which incorporated a bold "Roads to Resources", and frontier science program was to be funded by a re-chartered Bank of Canada. Diefenbaker's brilliant financing approach took a page from Alexander Hamilton and Lincoln's Greenback system which involved public bonds issued by Canada's National Bank in order to connect both old maturing WW2 Victory Bonds as well as new bonds directed towards Canada's development. Diefenbaker's vision for a true national credit system was encapsulated in his 1958 radio announcement:

*"This, the largest financial project in our history, offers an opportunity to all holders of victory bonds which were purchased as an act of patriotic faith during the war years, to re-invest them for the greater development of greater Canada. These monies that were advanced during the days of war, and which contributed to the victory, we now ask to be made available to speed the pace of peaceful progress and the program of national development... The action we are taking will make it possible for our nation to embark on a new era of peacetime prosperity far and beyond anything we have ever known."*

While this National Credit and Northern Vision program was sabotaged by a coordinated operation from London, Diefenbaker's strategy is just as applicable today as it was in 1958. Today Frobisher Bay plan remains the paragon of northern development, and complements the multi trillion dollar development policy of the Trans-Eurasian Belt Development which Russian Railways President Vladimir Yakunin described on March 23 2015, must be an *"interstate, inter-civilization, project. It should be an alternative to the current (neo-liberal) model, which has caused a systemic crisis. The project should be turned into a world 'future zone', and it must be based on leading, not catching, technologies."*

Today, Russia's Trans Eurasian Belt Development is fully integrated into China's "One Belt, One Road" program (aka: The New Silk Road), and provides a model upon which the Northern Vision can be re-awoken bringing Canada into alignment with the BRICS on arctic development, space and nuclear research.

**Projects that should have been...**
Bennett's rail (at left) was merely a stepping stone to his greater vision of a BC–Alaska railway through the Yukon (at right). Below right is a Federal design for the Frobisher Bay Domed city unveiled by John Diefenbaker in 1958

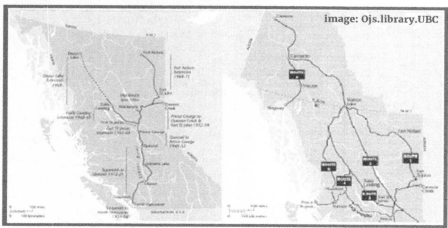

W.A.C Bennett

**Fig. 1:1958 Frobisher Bay Domed City design (commissioned by the Dept. of Public Works)**

John Diefenbaker

RUSSIA

Uelen
Alaska

Moscow    Yekaterinburg
London            Kazan
Berlin              Irkutsk
Paris

Trans-Eurasian
Belt Development

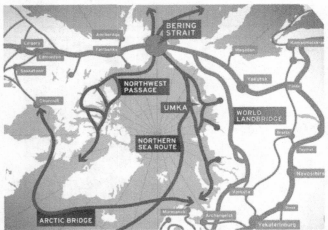

Above: Russia's Trans-Eurasian Development Belt proposed by the former Chief of Russian Railways Vladimir Yakunin (pictured below with President Putin). This project will come to play a major role in the internationalization of China's New Silk Road and broader Arctic policy for Canada.

Middle left: an Lpac produced diagram of rail and shipping routes across the Arctic

Bottom left: The Polar Star Icebreaker

# The Mid-Canada Development Corridor

While this program was rejected by the Liberal Government of 1969, which chose at that time to move Canada into a "post-industrial" paradigm, it has, since 2002 made a comeback under the sponsorship of former Liberal MP Rick Laliberte and a series of widely read articles published in the Walrus in Aug. 2016 instigated by architect John Von Nostrand working through the Northern Policy Institute.

Although General Richard Romer's 1967 design is presented within a false closed system paradigm of "resources exploitation", it is based upon a notion of permanent cities which would endure long after the original mineral which induced the town's creation is tapped. Within the context of the global New Silk Road, and Canada's arctic development strategy which necessarily blossoms from our participation in the Bering Strait tunnel, this program provides a valuable pathway for durable growth and is a far cry from the "temporary camp" model at the heart of the Alberta Tar sands in Fort McMurray.

In his 1970 book The Green North: Mid-Canada, Richard Rohmer stated the general intent of such a project in the following terms:

*"Wouldn't it be satisfying to know that we had a national goal, a national purpose for Canada? Such a goal exists in the creation of a second Canada"*

The original 1967 blueprint introduces a concept of permanent development in order to populate and integrate Canada's resource rich north with the rest of the nation. The original design sat upon a 4000 km rail track from Labrador through the northern provinces and into the Yukon which can naturally harmonize into the Alaska-Canada rail corridor and ultimately the Bering Strait rail connection which must drive this process.

In 2016, a team of scholars working out of the University of Calgary's School of Public Policy produced a study giving called "Planning for Infrastructure to Realize Canada's Potential: The Corridor Concept" . This study reviewed the feasibility of reviving the Mid-Canada Corridor in the 21st Century using a multi-modal process and would entirely transform Canada's economy both within its borders and as part of a global community of nations. The report describes the project in the following terms:

*"In initial concept, the Northern Corridor would be approximately 7000 km in length. It would largely follow the boreal forest in the northern part of the west, with a spur along the Mackenzie Valley, and then southeast from the Churchill area to northern Ontario and the "Ring of Fire" area; the corridor would then traverse northern Quebec to Labrador, with augmented ports. The right-of-way would have room for roads, rail lines, pipelines and transmission lines, and would interconnect with the existing (southern focused) transportation network."*

The authors of the report emphasized that the benefits of this project would not only loosen bottlenecks which currently exist in Canada's raw materials extraction and export sectors due to absence of northern infrastructure, while drastically improving the lives of northern communities which are currently isolated and suffer from a lack of jobs, as well as basic, affordable living standards.

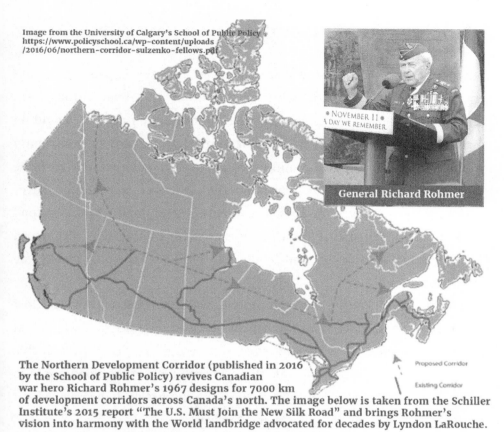

General Richard Rohmer

Proposed Corridor

Existing Corridor

The Northern Development Corridor (published in 2016
by the School of Public Policy) revives Canadian
war hero Richard Rohmer's 1967 designs for 7000 km
of development corridors across Canada's north. The image below is taken from the Schiller
Institute's 2015 report "The U.S. Must Join the New Silk Road" and brings Rohmer's
vision into harmony with the World landbridge advocated for decades by Lyndon LaRouche.

GATEWAY TO EURASIA:
## LINKING THE U.S. TO THE NEW SILK ROAD

# A Nuclear Renaissance

It is no exaggeration to say that without an intensive expansion of next generation nuclear fission, with an intention to break through on thermonuclear fusion at the soonest possible time, then not only could no great project in Canada ever be brought into being, but not even currently mediocre levels of production and potential relative population density be maintained. High energy flux density energy sources such as atomic power provides a clear gateway towards true wealth creation and was understood clearly by such Canadian nation builders as John Diefenbaker, CD Howe, W.A.C. Bennett, Jean Lesage and Daniel Johnson Sr. as the only viable way to build our nation.

Driving Arctic development at home, while reconstructing our lost infrastructure and manufacturing capabilities can only occur if we look at the global community with new eyes and recognize our most valuable technological contribution towards the new paradigm of development is to be found in this field. Currently, Canada's energy basket is heavily reliant on Hydro power, Coal, Natural gas and Nuclear.

That distribution must break from fossil fuels, and especially government-subsidized "green" energies, and into advanced 3rd and 4th generation nuclear with emphasis on cutting edge technologies.

As BRICS nations are vectoring their entire development strategy around a vigorous pursuit of nuclear energy, with over 70% of global nuclear energy development occurring in the BRICS nations or their allies, Canada must use its advanced nuclear technology not only to assist our global allies in everything from nuclear desalination to industrial nuclear power production, desalination and pure research. The Malthusian moratorium on nuclear energy pushed by Prince Philip, Maurice Strong, the Club of Rome and the 1001 Club since 1968 must now come to an end.

# Go For Fusion

Lastly, as the bubble of Canada's resource extraction economy pops, a vital change is needed now for not only Alberta, but all of Canada. A jewel exists in Canada's province of Alberta more precious than all the oil in the province. This jewel is located in the Alberta Fusion Energy Program (AFEP), affiliated with the Alberta Council of Technologies (ABCtech). Although this highly underfunded program is not yet at the forefront of Canadian energy policy, ABCtech under the leadership of Dr. Allan Offenburger, led an assessment team in 2014 to explore major fusion programs around the world and invited international fusion researchers to the Alberta Energy Forum in the Autumn of 2014 to present this bold potential to the political and business community.

Not a single pathway, but rather multiple pathways should be invested in if we are to make the breakthroughs necessary to make this energy source available for the benefit of humanity at the soonest possible date. Such pathways include Tokamaks as is being built in Switzerland, but also Stellarator, reversed field pinch, laser, dense plasma focus and tandem mirror methods. The pursuit of cold fusion should not be overlooked during this journey.

In a recent report, Lpac Science Research leader Ben Deniston made the point:

*"By increasing what the American economist Lyndon LaRouche has defined as the energy-flux density of the economy, we gain control over processes of higher energy throughput per unit of area, as expressed in a wide range of technologies, infrastructure projects, and production methods. With the fusion economy, energy supplies become relatively limitless, since the fusion fuel contained in one liter of seawater provides as much energy as 300 liters of petroleum".*

The Alberta Fusion Program serves as an inspiration for all other provinces which desperately need to participate in this cutting edge technology. Other provinces which had formerly had ambitious fusion programs such as Quebec's Tokamak at Varennes (cancelled in 1998) must therefore be under a revived federal Fusion Energy Canada program which had been shut down at that same time.

Alongside revived provincial and federal fusion programs working with the world nuclear community, Canada's universities must be united and reformed around the same endeavor. Currently, only seven universities have active fusion research programs, but this must expand in quantity and quality coordinated with the private sector such as the British Columbia-based General Fusion Inc., under the umbrella of a reformed National Reseach Council (NRC) and renationalized Atomic Energy Canada Ltd. (AECL) following the model of Canada's "Minister of Everything" C.D. Howe from 1945-1958.

Given the fact that next-generation nuclear fission, breakthroughs in Fusion and mining Helium-3 on the moon are at the center of China's economic policy and is the basis of the now globally-established BRICS alliance, adopting such a pro-fusion outlook for Canada's energy policy would immediately propel Canada out of its backwardness as a raw materials exporter and into a pro-industrial dynamic centered on true anti-entropic global development.

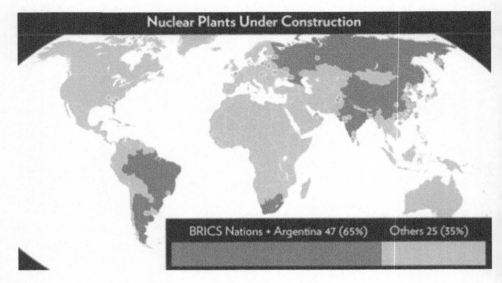

## Nuclear Plants Under Construction

BRICS Nations + Argentina 47 (65%)    Others 25 (35%)

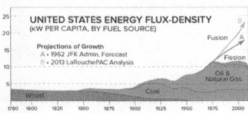

### UNITED STATES ENERGY FLUX-DENSITY
(kW PER CAPITA, BY FUEL SOURCE)

Projections of Growth
A • 1962 JFK Admin. Forecast
B • 2013 LaRouchePAC Analysis

Fusion
Fission
Oil & Natural Gas
Coal
Wood

Progress is not a choice, but an existential necessity for all life.

Featured above: the 2015 overview of nuclear plants under construction. Other images feature the scientific conection between population growth and the increase of the energy-flux-density of the system.

Nuclear power represents the densest form of energy currently available to mankind and is instrumental as we open our minds to the need to explore space and develop the earth simultaneously.

All images were produced by the Schiller Institute

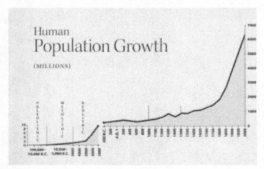

### Human Population Growth
(MILLIONS)

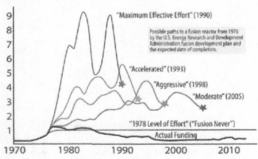

"Maximum Effective Effort" (1990)

Possible paths to a fusion reactor from 1976 by the U.S. Energy Research and Development Administration fusion development plan and the expected date of completion.

"Accelerated" (1993)

"Aggressive" (1998)

"Moderate" (2005)

"1978 Level of Effort" ("Fusion Never")
Actual Funding

| How Much Fuel of Different Types Provides the Same Amount of Energy as a Tank of Gas? | |
|---|---|
| FUEL SOURCE | AMOUNT OF FUEL |
| Combustion of Wood | 300 Pounds |
| Combustion of Coal | 200 Pounds |
| Combustion of Gas | 16 Gallons (Gas Tank) |
| Typical Nuclear Fuel | 1 Paperclip* |
| Deuterium-Tritium Fusion | 1 Grain of Rice* |
| Matter-Antimatter Reaction | 1 Flea Egg* |

*  Equivalent amount of weight (To provide the same amount of energy as an average tank of gasoline, more or less weight of various different fuel types is required, because of their differing energy densities. The value for typical nuclear fuel would be significantly higher with the use of reprocessing and breeder reactors.)

# The North American Water and Power Alliance

The title "NAWAPA" refers to the proposal for a North American Water and Power Alliance, to bring water that flows from the rivers of Alaska and Canada into the sea, southward into the Canadian Prairies providing agriculture, power projects, shipping and also a cleaning of the polluted Great Lakes. It also would bring water to the driest areas of the United States and Mexico. Originally drafted in 1964, NAWAPA was never built, for political reasons. But with the scorching droughts of recent years, it is more urgent than ever.

We publish here the beginning and the end of the video of a 2012 Lpac educational video on the project.

We live on a continent whose western part has a wide discrepancy of rainfall distribution due to the particularities of the Pacific Ocean weather system. The area stretching from Alaska and Yukon down to Washington State has 40 times the annual river runoff of the Southwest and Northern Mexico.

To move some of this runoff to areas where there is little, it appears at first glance that a very long canal or pipeline would be required. Closer inspection shows that such a canal is already built! More specifically, there is a continuous stretch of naturally made canals, in the form of Rocky Mountain trenches and valleys, stretching from southeast Alaska through southern Idaho, roughly 2,000 miles.

All that is required is the construction of 31 dams, and a 2,000-mile route utilizing these topographical features can deliver 11% of the runoff water of Alaska, British Columbia, and Yukon to bring a new source of surface water to the U.S. Southwest and Mexico, that will last as long as the rain continues to fall in the northern mountains of the continent, an amount capable of doubling food production, saving cities, farms, and industries across the Southwest, and securing livelihoods for generations to come. The construction of the northern storage and power system will bring with it the independence and industrialization of Alaska, the rapid development of British Columbia, and the general development of the continent as a whole. Implementing the project will save and revive vital industries and technological capabilities, and create millions of long-term, productive jobs.

# NAWAPA & Transportation Corridors

Returning to Canada, a major addition to the main storage route described integrates with the proposed development of British Columbia and supplies the Canadian prairies with needed water. Peace River runoff and other Mackenzie Basin streams, as well as potential flows from the runoff of the far North, would make possible a barge canal across Canada, connecting existing rivers with a 730-footwide canal large enough for barges, stretching from the man-made Williston Lake, created by B.C. Premier W.A.C. Bennett, all the way to Lake Superior. Sufficient water supplies will be drawn from the canal for the needs of Alberta, Saskatchewan, and Manitoba, and a branching barge canal will cross through the Dakotas and link up with the Missouri and Mississippi river systems, designed for flood control as well as for shipping and irrigation.

The seaway will stabilize the levels of the Great Lakes when excess water is available. Branching off from the canal, a seaway between Lake Winnipeg and Hudson Bay, and a canal between Georgian Bay and James Bay would create cheap transport routes for resource development. The extension of waterways into areas where existing access is achieved only by expensive overland transport, will open vast new areas to accelerated settlement and development.

Barge traffic connecting Lake Williston to a navigable Fraser River, through locks near Prince George, would make British Columbia an inflection point for world trade, and allow for material processing within the province, making use of the extensive 32 GW of surplus hydro-power possible through the system.

For the efficient construction of the NAWAPA XXI reservoirs, canals, pumping and power stations, the completion of the Alaskan-Canadian rail system, studied under former Alaskan Gov. Frank Murkowski, is immediately available for construction during the design, pre-construction, and site preparation phases of NAWAPA XXI.

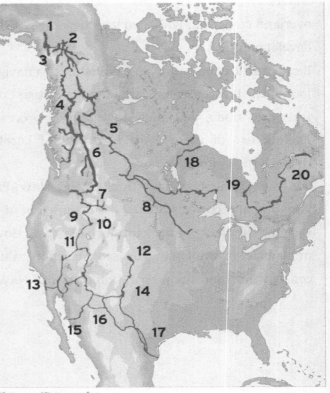

# REGIONAL
## BREAKDOWN

1. Susitna Reservoir
2. Yukon Reservoir
3. Copper Reservoir
4. Taku Lift
5. Canadian/Great-Lakes Waterway
6. Rocky Mountain Trench
7. Sawtooth Lifts
8. Dakota Waterway
9. Sawtooth Tunnel
10. Great Basin Waterway
11. Lake Nevada
12. Colorado Reservoir
13. Baja Aqueduct
14. Colorado Aqueduct
15. Sonora Aqueduct
16. Chihuahua Aqueduct
17. Rio-Grande Aqueduct
18. Hudson Bay Seaway
19. James Bay Seaway
20. Knob Lake Barge Canal

**Above:**
A regional breakdown of the 20 greatest components to the North American Water and Power Alliance which will profoundly transform North America's water cycles and open a new age in biospheric engineering.

**To the left:**
a map featuring both NAWAPA as well as two major Mexican water diversion projects known as the PLHINO and PLHIGON which divert water from the flood-prone south towards the drought prone north.

Both images courtesy of LaRouchepac

# The Fallacy of "Canadian Development" that must be corrected

The biggest problem with the Bennett design, supporters of Sir John A. Macdonald's National Policy, Diefenbaker's Northern Vision and Rohmer's Mid-Canada plan, is that they are all couched in the closed false nationalist matrix of "Canada first, we'll see what happens after we build it second". Compare that to the December 2007 keynote address by Lyndon LaRouche to Canadians at the *Canada and the Coming Eurasian World* Ottawa Conference regarding how we have to re-conceptualize our definition of "sovereignty" around the *Treaty of Westphalia* and the global system of mutual interest being now being created:

*"If we love mankind, and can love the benefit given to the other nation, what are doing that's good for them? If we can think in those terms, then we will get away from the dog-eat-dog tendency which we've seen again, lately, and get back to the idea that we are not animals; we do not breed progeny. We develop human beings, and we hope that the next generation will have a life better than ours, because we've made that improvement possible."*

Acting on this highest level of sovereignty means breaking the sacred cow established with Sir John A. Macdonald's CPR rail programs that rooted our tradition of great projects deeply within a British geopolitical agenda-keeping us only strong enough to not be absorbed by the American System or influenced by the Russians. In the new era that is now being shaped by the future-orientation led by the China's Silk Road and the new Eurasian paradigm, this tragic colonial mentality and false sense of Canadian nationalism must be superseded by a higher principle.

# ICBMS AND THE DEATH OF THE AVRO ARROW

Today, John Diefenbaker is most popularly  remembered as the man who killed Canada's Avro Arrow in 1959. The Avro was the world's first supersonic jet, and the Canadian made engineering genius that created these machines was the envy of the world. Due to the existence of this aerospace program's success, Canadian engineers filled the majority of the positions in NASA under Presidents Eisenhower and Kennedy. While it is a tragedy that such a program met the sad fate which it did, the circumstances of its demise under Diefenbaker's watch must be understood not only as having occurred within the context developed in the main report, but also within the framework of the same geopolitical tension that brought them into existence in the first place.

Today, historians rarely mention the important fact that the Avro jets were the creation of a contract for the US military in order to deploy nuclear warheads upon enemy territory within the quickest possible time frame. With the advent of Intercontinental Ballistic Missiles (ICBMs), the speed of warhead delivery dramatically outpaced Avro's potential, making their production obsolete for that purpose. Without the continued American contracts, and since no other contracts from other nations were forthcoming, the means were no longer available to continue the program. On February 20 1959, Diefenbaker announced Avro's discontinuation.

To the shock of all, 14,525 personnel were disbanded at once, all designs, blueprints, models and pictures were destroyed and the only Avro jets in existence were immediately cut down into scrap metal.

# NOTES

# Preface footnotes

[1] Pierre Beaudry's referenced work can be found in Canada: Republic or Colony, Reproduced in the Canadian Patriot Special Report 2012

[2] Graham Lowry, How the Nation Was Won: America's Untold Story 1630-1754, 1988

[3] Anton Chaitkin, Treason in America: From Aaron Burr to Averill Harimann, 1985

[4] Bob Ingraham, Manhattan's Struggle for Human Freedom Against the Slave Power of Virginia, EIR May 8, 2015

[5] Allen Salisbury, The Civil War and the American System: America's Battle With Britain 1860-1876, 1st printing. 1978

# Chapter I

[2] Benjamin Kizer, "*The Northwest Pacific Planning Project*", December 1942, p.5

[3] An irony of Canadian history is that in large measure, the federal government, unlike the U.S example, has been largely responsible for prohibiting and sabotaging the aspirations of its provinces to develop, while the responsibility has customarily fallen to the shoulders of bold premiers to lead Ottawa to the future by the nose

[4] W.A.C. Bennett interviewed by David Mitchell, 18 June 1977,1675-23, track 2, p. 4, BCARS

[5] In exposing the agendas of subversive agencies (witting or not), Bennett frequently commented that "there are two type of people in the world: those that get things done, and those who throw sand on the gears"

[6] *Conversations with WAC Bennett*, Methune Press, Toronto, 1980.pg 107-108 (heretofore "Conversations)

[7] McNaughton would later go onto lead the fight against the North American Power Alliance, becoming the primary organizer against the proposal and its champion, Senator Frank Moss.

[8] On several occasions, the potential for Canada's annexation into the USA had nearly materialized beginning with the Quebec Act of 1774 effectively blocking Canada's entry into the anti-imperial struggle of the 13 colonies, followed by the failed 1776 takeover by Benedict Arnold. After this point, the greatest threat to the imperial control over the Dominion of Canada would be located in the concept of the "custom's union" modelled on the German "Zollverein" industrial development model of Frederick List. This model would be advanced by Isaac Buchanan in 1865, Sir Wilfred Laurier until 1911, and would again re-emerge as a failed attempt again in 1945. The Customs Union view would have given Canada privileges enjoyed by the U.S. states amongst themselves under the principled guidance of the U.S. Constitution and its anti-monetarist essence.

[9] *Conversations*, p.111

[10] "*I don't think there is any question that the Coyne Affair was the destruction of the Diefenbaker government right then and there*"- Alvin Hamilton, *The Value of a "Coyne": The Diefenbaker Government and the 1961 Coyne Affair*, Daniel Macfarlane, University of Ottawa, 2008. p 140

[11] *Conversations*, p. 112

[12] *Conversations*, p 116

[13] BC Studies, Winter 1975-76, A Study in Regional Strategy: The Alaska, B.C., Yukon Conferences, by P.R. Johannsen, p.29

[14] Funds totaling six million dollars were raised privately, concluding the project to connect the continents by rail across the Bering Strait could be done for $300 million. An editorial in the New York Times of October

24th, 1905, observed that "the Bering Strait Tunnel is a project which at some time in the future is likely to command a great deal of very purposeful consideration."

[15] The anti-NAFTA logic wielded by Bennett is evidenced in a statement from May 1956:

*"As a Government, we must safeguard vital interests of our people, and we must assure that adequate supplies of power are available for our own present and future requirements. However, we are also fully aware of the needs and requirements of our good friends to the south insofar as power is concerned, just as I am sure that they are cognizant of our needs, for example, of an outlet to the Pacific through the Alaskan Panhandle. If the interests of both parties are understood, then certainly a mutually satisfactory arrangement can be reached."*

[16] *A Study in Regional Strategy*, p 43

[17] Hon. R. A. Williams, Minister of Lands, Forests and Water Resources, interviewed on CBC "Hourglass" television program, 18 December 1973

[18] In describing their history on the website www.naturetrust.bc.ca, we can read the motivation for the conservation areas of BC: *"There was also a sense of urgency in getting the projects underway because BC was experiencing a period of rapid growth and industrial development. That is how The National Second Century Fund of British Columbia, later to be called The Nature Trust of British Columbia, was born."*

# Chapter II

[1] *The Beastmen Behind the Dropping of the Atomic Bomb* by Leo Wolfe, 21st Century Science and Technology, vol 18 no. 1, p. 22

[2] Cara Spittal, *The Diefenbaker Moment*, University of Toronto Thesis, 2011

[3] American capital invested into Canada would increase from $6.9 billion to $13.5 billion during this period

[4] The fight would erupt when it became evident that B.C. Electric would attempt to sabotage Bennett's vision of developing northern B.C with revenue from the Columbia River Treaty. Bennett would oversee B.C. Electric's takeover by the province.

[5] Spencer Cross, *Who We Fight episode 3: The Organization Children* LaRouchePacTV, 2012, www.larouchepac.com/node/20935

[6] Under a parliamentary system, no minority government will do for any government which hopes to achieve anything, since any mandate proposed by that government could be overthrown by a coalition of opposition parties, and the government could easily fall at any time via a vote of "no confidence" and new elections spontaneously called

[7] Albert Gervais, *Daniel Johnson: A Short Biography*, pg. 18

[8] Carrigan, *Canadian Party Platforms*, pg 226-232

[9] Diefenbaker, *Memoires* vol.2, p. 286

[10] Diefenbaker, *Memoires* vol 2 pg. 270

[11] Peter Newman, *Renegade in Power*, pg. 303

[12] It is interesting to note that CIIA affiliated economist and Walter Gordon ally Wynne Plumptre was the only official from the Ministry of Finance's office attending the Feb. 15 board meeting that voted on the pension increase. Plumptre neglected to inform either the Minister of Finance or Deputy Minister of Finance of the occurrence.

[13] *Past Imperfect*, p. 131

[14] *Past Imperfect*, p.136

[15] Canadian wheat sales to China skyrocketed from $12 million dollars in 1959 to $137.3 million in 1962. Breaking "trading with the enemy" laws,

the USA attempted blocking the use of equipment vital for wheat exports leased from American firms when Diefenbaker threatened to go on radio and say that the USA was attempting to run the Canadian economy. JFK acquiesced and trade proceeded..

[16] Diefenbaker, *Memoirs*, p.49

[17] Diefenbaker, *Memoirs*, p.53

[18] Azzi, *Walter Gordon and Rise of Canadian Nationalism*, McGill-QueensUniversity Press, 1999, pg. 7


# Chapter III

[1] While 60% of Canadians thought American investment should continue in 1950, that number had fallen to a mere 30% by 1957

# Chapter IV

[1] p.1-2 *A Short History of Crown Agents and Their Office*, by Arthur William Abbott, C.M.G, C.B.E The Chiswick Press 1959. — A.W. Abbott à été Secrétaire de Crown Agents de 1954 à 1958.

[2] p. 45 *Renée Lévesque: Portrait d'un Québécois*, par Jean Provencher Éd. La Presse 1973

[3] In order to win the war, Roosevelt created the OWI and OSS (Office of Strategic Services). OWI took care of the propaganda while OSS took care of intelligence. After the war the OSS and OWI were dismantled, as they were not entirely under American control. The OSS became the CIA and the OWI was re-integrated into British Intelligence services.

[4] p. 71 *Renée Lévesque: Portrait d'un Québécois*, par Jean Provencher Éd. La Presse 1973

[5] At the end of the 1950s, 60% of Québec's students were studying in science programs, and 50% of Canada's hydroelectric power was generated in Québec. By the beginning of the 1960s, Hydro Québec forecasted that 50% of its energy would come from nuclear power by 1985. In 1963, under the direction of Alexander King (later to go on to co found the Club of Rome, in which Maurice Strong would be a key member), the Organization of Economic Cooperation and Development (OECD) had produced a report which served as a model for a "educational reform" within all industrialized countries. Some of these reforms would involve replacing constructive geometry for "new math", and replacing the study of Greek and Latin with French existentialism. In Quebec, this reform coincided with the creation of the Ministry of Education (which involved a battle between the Catholic church and Freemasonry). See La Présse of November 11, 1963- A five part series defending the Grand Lodge of Quebec.

[6] The Symphony Program was a Franco-German project consisting of two communications satellites which would have the effect of connecting Quebec with the rest of the French speaking world. De Gaulle invited Quebec to participate with Johnson replying "the cosmos will speak French". The project wouldn't be ready until the beginning of the 1970s. Sadly, the Ariane rockets had exploded on lift off twice and were finally sent in space by the American Delta rocket in 1974 and 1975. However the Americans only cooperated on the condition that there would be no intercontinental link, thus immediately excluding Quebec from the project.

[7] p. 249 *Daniel Johnson: 1964-1968 la difficile recherche de l'égalité.* Pierre Godin, Edition de l'homme,1980.

[8] Matthew Ehret-Kump, *Diefenbaker and the Sabotage of the Northern Vision*, The Canadian Patriot, CRC, January 2013, p. 28

[9] Albert Gervais, *Daniel Johnson: A Short Biography*, pg. 18

[10] John Diefenbaker, *Memoirs* vol. 2, Macmillan of Canada, Toronto, p.94

# Chapter V

[1] Premier Bennett fought for almost 7 years to ensure that his plans to develop the Peace River in northern BC would not be sabotaged by either Mcnaughton or Fulton who tried various schemes to ensure that Canada was not brought into closer proximity with America to the north or the south. For more, see `W.A.C Bennett: Canada`s Spritual Father to NAWAPA`, by this author in The Canadian Patriot #4, Jan 2013

# Chapter VI

[1] General Bernard Montgomery writing about the Dieppe Raid in his autobiography, *The Memoirs of Field Marshal Montgomery* (1958), cited in http://www.spartacus.schoolnet.co.uk/2WWdieppe.htm

[2] *Six Years of War, The Official History of the Canadian Army in the Second World War Chapter X*, p. 321 [http://www.ibiblio.org/hyperwar/UN/Canada/CA/SixYears/SixYears–10.html

[3] McNaughton. John Swettenham, The Ryerson Press, 1968. Vol. 1, p. 278 n: "Royal" gave the title a derogatory military flavor; "Twenty" referred to the twenty-cent allowance.

[4] loc. cit., p. 271

[5] Swettenham, loc. cit., p. 285

[6] http://saskfiles.com/35july2page1.pdf

[7] A report put out by the Western Canadian-American assembly in 1964 said: *"Canada and the United States are moving in the direction of a new and significant policy for the development of energy resources particularly water power on a continental scale. Recent technological advances which have made the border increasingly irrelevant have brought about in both countries the willingness to consider an encouraging degree of integration."* Swettenham, p. 332, n.

[8] *Water Resources of Canada*, University of Toronto Press, 1967, p. 22.

[9] Montreal Gazette, April 12, 1967. section A5

# Chapter VII

[1] *Time To Stop and Think, A Brief to PM Trudeau*, The Canadian Coalition for Nuclear Responsibility, 1977

[2] The Anglo-Dutch governance of the WWF was established by the Prince of the Netherlands, Prince Bernhard and Prince Philip, of Great Britain. The second WWF president replacing Bernhard was none other than John Louden, the former head of Royal Dutch Shell. Louden was also a member of the 1001 Club.

[3] Jeff Steinberg, *Montreal Permindex Ties Revealed to JFK Murder*, 1001 Club, the Canadian Patriot #5, 2013, downloadable at http://canadianpatriot.org/?p=476

Made in the USA
Monee, IL
16 April 2021